BARBARA

junie b. jones®

and a Little Monkey Business

2

540L

illustrated by
Denise
Brunkus

Long tail Books

Barbara Park was best-known as the creator and author of the New York Times bestselling *Junie B. Jones* series, the stories of an outrageously funny kindergartener who has kept kids and their grown ups laughing—and reading—for over two decades. Every bit as funny and as outrageous as her best-known character, Barbara Park originally intended to become a high school teacher but decided to express her sense of humor through writing. Since her first book, *Don't Make Me Smile*, was published in 1981, the author went on to write over fifty books and won more than forty children's book awards, including several Children's Choice Awards. Park died in 2013, but her legacy lives on in the laughter her books give to readers all over the world.

Denise Brunkus has illustrated more than 60 books, most notably the *Junie B. Jones* series written by Barbara Park. She also illustrated *READ ALL ABOUT IT!*, written by former First Lady Laura Bush and her daughter Jenna Bush, which went on to become a New York Times Bestseller. Her books have also been recognized with numerous state reading awards, including the Young Hoosier Picture Book Award.

junie b. jones®
and a Little Monkey Business

by BARBARA PARK

illustrated by
Denise Brunkus

Long tail Books

To Cal and Nate,
the cutest little monkeys
their grammy ever saw!

Junie B. Jones and a Little Monkey Business by Barbara Park

This bilingual edition was published by Longtail Books in 2021 by arrangement with Barbara Park c/o Writers House LLC through KCC(Korea Copyright Center Inc.), Seoul.

ISBN 979-11-91343-09-0 14740

Longtail Books

Contents

1
Surprise

My name is Junie B. Jones. The B **stands for** Beatrice. **Except** I don't like Beatrice. I just like B and **that's all**. B stands for something else, too.

B stands for B-A-B-Y.

I'm only in **kindergarten**. But I already know how to **spell** B-A-B-Y. That's because my mother told me that she is going to have one of those things.

She and Daddy told me about it at dinner one night. It was the night we had **stew**ed tomatoes[1]—which I hate very much.

"Daddy and I have a surprise for you,

1 **stewed tomatoes** 토마토 스튜. 고기에 버터와 조미료를 넣고, 잘게 썬 토마토와 다른 채소를 섞어 뭉근히 익혀서 만드는 서양식 요리.

Junie B.," said Mother.

And so then I got very happy inside. Because maybe I didn't have to eat my stewie pewie tomatoes.[2]

And also sometimes a surprise means a

---

2 **stewie pewie tomatoes** 주니 B.가 '역겨운 토마토 스튜'라는 의미로 만든 말장난. 스튜 요리를 뜻하는 'stewed'와 역겨움을 나타내는 표현 'pew(P.U.)'를 변형해 'tomatoes' 앞에 붙였다.

present! And presents are my very favorite things in the whole world!

I **bounce**d up and down on my chair.

"What is it? Is it all **wrap**ped up? I don't see it," I said very excited.

Then I looked under the table. Because maybe the surprise was hiding down there with a red ribbon on top of it.

Mother and Daddy smiled at each other. Then Mother held my hand.

"Junie B., how would you like to have a little baby brother or sister?" she said.

I made my shoulders go up and down.

"I don't know. Maybe," I told her.

Then I looked under my chair.

"Guess what?" I said. "I can't find that **silly** willy[3] present anywhere."

Mother made me sit up. Then she and my daddy said some more **stuff** about a baby.

"The baby will be yours, too, Junie B.," Daddy said. "Just think. You'll have your very own little brother or sister to play with. Won't that be fun?"

I did my **shoulder**s up and down again. "I don't know. Maybe," I said.

Then I got down from my chair and ran into the living room.

"BAD NEWS, **FELLAS**!" I **holler**ed very loud. "THE PRESENT ISN'T IN THIS **DUMB** BUNNY[4] ROOM, EITHER!"

Mother and Daddy came into the

---

3 **silly willy** 어리석은 사람이나 바보 같은 물건을 이르는 말.

4 **dumb bunny** 좀 모자라거나 우직한 사람을 이르는 속어적 표현.

living room. They didn't look that **smiley** anymore.

Daddy took a big breath. "There is no *present,* Junie B.," he said. "We never said we had a present. We said we had a *surprise*. Remember?"

Then Mother sat down next to me. "The surprise is that I'm going to have a *baby,* Junie B. In a few months you're going to have a little baby brother or sister. Do you get what I'm saying yet?"

Just then I **fold**ed my arms and **made a grumpy face**. 'Cause **all of a sudden** I got it, that's why.

"You didn't get me a darned[5] thing, did

---

5 **darned** 'damn(빌어먹을)'을 순화한 단어로, 못마땅하거나 짜증스러울 때 쓰는 표현.

you?" I said very **growly**.

Mother looked angry at me. "I **give up**!" she said. Then she went back into the kitchen.

Daddy said that I **owe**d her a **'pology**.

A 'pology is when I have to say the words *I'm sorry*.

"Yes, but she owes me a 'pology, too," I said. "Because a baby isn't a very good surprise."

I made a **wrinkly** nose. "Babies smell like P.U.[6]," I explained. "I smelled one at my friend Grace's house. It had some **spit-up** on its front. And so I held my nose and hollered, 'P.U.! WHAT A **STINK**

---

6 **P.U.** '어휴'라는 뜻으로 어떤 냄새나 악취가 날 때 혐오감 혹은 역겨움을 나타내는 표현.

BOMB![7]' And then that Grace made me go home."

After I finished my story, Daddy went into the kitchen to talk to Mother.

Then Mother called me in there. And she said if the baby smells like a stink bomb, she will buy me my very own **air freshener**. And I can **spray** the can all **by myself**.

Except not on the P.U. baby.

"I would like the one that smells as fresh as a Carolina[8] **pine** forest," I said.

Then me and Mother **hug**ged. And I sat back down at the table. And I finished

---

7 **stink bomb** 방귀 폭탄. 누르면 방귀와 같은 냄새가 나는 장난감.

8 **Carolina** 노스 캐롤라이나(North Carolina). 미국 대서양 연안 중부에 있는 주(州)로, 주도(州都)는 롤리(Raleigh)이며 섬유 공업과 펄프·제지 공업이 발달해 있다.

eating my dinner.

Except not my stewie pewie tomatoes.

And so guess what?

No **dessert**, that's what.

2
The Dumb Baby's Room

Mother and Daddy **fix**ed up a room for the new baby. It's called a **nursery**. **Except** I don't know why. Because a baby isn't a nurse, of course.

The baby's room used to be the guest room. That's where all our guests used to sleep. Only we never had much guests.

And so now if we get some, they'll have to sleep on a table or something.

The baby's room has new **stuff** in it. That's because Mother and Daddy went shopping at the new baby stuff store.

They bought a new baby **dresser** with green and yellow **knob**s on it. And a new baby lamp with a giraffe on the lamp **shade**. And also, a new **rock**ing chair for when the baby cries and you can't shut it up.

And there's a new baby **crib**, too.

A crib is a bed with **bar**s on the side of it. It's kind of like a **cage** at the zoo. Except with a crib, you can put your hand through the bars. And the baby won't pull you in and kill you.

And guess what else is in the nursery? **Wallpaper**, that's what! The **jungle** kind.

With pictures of elephants, and lions, and a big fat hippo-pot-of-something.[1]

And there's monkeys, too! Which are my most favorite[2] jungle guys in the whole world!

Mother and Daddy **paste**d on the wallpaper together.

Me and my dog Tickle were watching them.

"This wallpaper looks very cute in here," I told them. "I would like some of it in my room, too, I think. Okay?" I said. "Can I? Can I?"

---

1 **hippo-pot-of-something** 'hippopotamus(하마)'라는 단어가 완전히 기억나지 않아 얼버무린 말.

2 **most favorite** '가장 좋아하는'이라는 뜻을 지닌 비격식적인 표현. 원래는 단어 'favorite'이 '선호하는'이라는 의미를 나타내기 때문에 형용사 최상급을 만드는 부사인 'most'를 잘 붙이지 않는다.

"We'll see," said Daddy.

We'll see is another word for no.

"Yeah, only that's not **fair**," I said. "'Cause the baby gets all new **junk** and I have all old junk."

"Poor Junie B.," said Mother very **teasing**.

Then she **bended**[3] down and tried to **hug** me. Only she couldn't do it very good. Because of her big fat **stomach**—which is where the stupid baby is.

"I don't think I'm going to like this dumb baby," I said.

Mother stopped hugging me.

---

3 **bended** (bent) 영어권 국가의 아이들이 동사의 과거형을 말할 때 모든 단어의 끝에 '-ed'를 붙이는 실수를 종종 한다. 이 책에 나오는 'holded(held)', 'runned(run)' 등이 이와 같은 경우이다.

"Don't say that, Junie B. Of course you will," she said.

"Of course I won't," I talked back. "Because it won't even let me hug you very good. And anyway, I don't even know its stupid dumb name."

Then Mother sat down in the new rocking chair. And she tried to put me on her **lap**. Only I wouldn't **fit**. So she just holded my hand.

"That's because Daddy and I haven't picked a name for the baby yet," she explained. "We want a name that's a little bit different. You know, something cute like Junie B. Jones. A name that people will remember."

And so I thought and thought very

hard. And then I **clap**ped my hands together real loud.

"Hey! I know one!" I said very excited. "It's the **cafeteria** lady at my school. And her name is Mrs. Gutzman!"

Mother **frown**ed a little bit. And so maybe she didn't hear me, I think.

"MRS. GUTZMAN!" I **holler**ed. "That's a cute name, don't you think? And I remembered it, too! Even after I only heard it one time, Mrs. Gutzman **stick**ed right in my head!"

Mother took a big breath. "Yes, honey. But I'm not sure that Mrs. Gutzman is a good name for a **tiny** baby."

And so then I **scrunch**ed my face up. And I thought and thought all over again.

"How 'bout **Teeny**?" I said. "Teeny would be good."

Mother smiled. "Well, Teeny might be cute while the baby was little. But what would we call him when he grows up?"

"Big Teeny!" I called out very happy.

Then Mother said, "We'll see."

Which means no Big Teeny.

After that, I didn't feel so happy anymore.

"When's this dumb bunny baby getting here anyway?" I said.

Mother frowned again. "The baby is not a dumb bunny, Junie B.," she said. "And it will be here very soon. So I think you'd better start **get**ting **used to** the idea."

Then her and Daddy began pasting

wallpaper again.

And so I opened the new baby dresser with the green and yellow knobs. And I looked at the new baby clothes.

The baby **pajamas** were very **weensy**. And the baby socks wouldn't even fit on my big **piggie toe**.

"I'm going to be the **boss** of this baby," I said to Tickle. "'Cause I'm the biggest, that's why."

Daddy **snap**ped his fingers at me. "That's enough of that kind of talk, missy,[4]" he said.

Missy's my name when I'm in trouble.

After that, him and Mother went to the

---

4 **missy** '아가씨'라는 뜻으로 화나 애정을 담아 어린 여성을 부르는 표현.

kitchen to get some more paste.

And so I looked down the **hall** to make sure he was gone.

"Yeah, only I'm still gonna be the boss of it," I **whisper**ed.

Ha ha. So there.

3
A Very Wonderful Thing!

Yesterday a very wonderful thing happened!

And it's called—I had pie[1] for dinner!

Just pie and **that's all**!

That's because my mother went to the hospital to have the baby. And Daddy and

---

1 **pie** 파이. 밀가루와 버터 반죽 위에 과일 또는 고기 등을 넣고 구워서 만드는 서양 디저트.

2 **grampa** '할아버지(grandpa)'를 부르는 말로, 'gramp', 'grampa', 'grampy' 등 다양한 표현이 있다.

Grandma Miller went with her.

And so me and my grampa[2] got to stay at his house. All **by ourselves**. And no one even **babysit**ted us!

And guess what? Grampa **smoke**d a

real live cigar[3] right inside the house! And Grandma didn't **yell**, "Go outside with that thing, Frank!"

After that, my grampa gave me a piggyback **ride**.[4]

And he let me put on Grandma Miller's new hat—with the long brown **feather**.

And also, I got to walk in her red high **heel**s.

Only then I fell down in the kitchen. And so I quick **took** them **off**.

"Hey! I could **crack** my head open in these dumb things," I said very loud.

After that, I opened up the **'frigerator**.

---

3 **cigar** 시가. 담뱃잎을 썰지 않고 통째로 돌돌 말아서 만든 담배.

4 **piggyback ride** 업기 또는 목말 태우기. 등에 업어 주거나 업히는 것을 뜻한다.

'Cause I was hungry from playing, that's why.

"HEY! GUESS WHAT? THERE'S A BIG FAT LEMON PIE IN HERE, FRANK!" I hollered.

And so then Grampa Miller got down two plates. And then me and him ate the big fat lemon pie for our dinner!!

Just pie and that's all!!

And we're not even going to get in trouble! 'Cause we're going to tell Grandma that her cat ate it!

And here's another very fun thing. I got to sleep in Grampa Miller's guest room!

First I put on my **p.j.'s** with the feet in them. And then my grampa watched me **brush** my new **front tooth**. And he

tucked me into the big guest bed.

"Sweet dreams, Junie B.," he said.

Except for then I got a little bit of **scare**d in me.

"Yeah. Only guess what, Grampa," I said. "It's very dark in this big room. And so there might be hidey[5] things in here."

Grampa looked all around the room. And also in the **closet**.

"Nope. No hidey things in here," he said.

After that he left on the **hall** light for me. So my **'magination** wouldn't **run wild**.

---

5 **hidey** 주니 B.가 만들어 낸 단어로 동사 'hide(숨다)'의 뒤에 '-y'를 붙여 '숨은, 숨어 있는'이라는 의미의 형용사로 사용하였다. 이 책에 나오는 'pumpy', 'frowny', 'shouty' 등도 이와 같은 경우이다.

Except I still didn't sleep that good. 'Cause there was a **drooly** guy with **claw**s under my bed, I think.

And so this morning, my eyes felt very **sag**ging.

Only then I **sniff**ed something that woke them right up.

And its name was delicious waffles![6]

Grampa Miller cooked them for me! And he let me **pour** on my own syrup.[7] And he didn't yell whoa! whoa! whoa!

After that, me and him played until it was time for **kindergarten**.

---

6 **waffle** 와플. 밀가루, 달걀, 우유, 설탕 등을 섞은 반죽을 격자 무늬 틀에 넣어 구운 것으로, 잼이나 버터 등을 얹어 먹는다.

7 **syrup** 시럽. 여러 가지 과일의 즙에 설탕을 섞은 뒤 녹여 만든 걸쭉한 액체로, 과자나 음료를 만들 때 사용하거나 음식에 뿌려 먹는다.

8 **funnest** 형용사 'fun'의 최상급을 잘못 만든 것으로, 올바른 표현은 'most fun'이다.

Except before I left, the funnest[8] thing of all happened! My grandma Miller came home!

And she said that Mother had a baby!

And it was the boy kind!

Then me and her and my grampa all did a big **giant** hug!

And Grandma Miller picked me up. And she **swing**ed me in the air.

"You're just going to love him, Junie B.!" she said. "Your new brother is the cutest little monkey I've ever seen!"

Then my eyes got very wide. "He is? Really?" I said.

Grandma Miller put me down. Then she started talking to my grampa.

"Wait till you see him, Frank," she said.

"He's got the longest little fingers and **toe**s!"

I **tug**ged on her dress. "How long, Grandma?" I said. "Longer than mine?"

But Grandma just kept on talking.

"And his hair, Frank! My word![9] He's got **oodles** and oodles of thick black hair!"

I pulled on Grandma's arm. "How come, Grandma? How come he's got hair?" I asked. "I thought little babies **were supposed to** be **baldies**."

But still, my grandma didn't answer me.

"And he's big, too, Frank. He's much bigger than any of the other babies in the

---

9 **my word** '이런' 또는 '아이고'라는 의미로 놀랐을 때 쓰는 표현.

hospital. And you should feel how tightly he **grab**s on to your finger when you—"

Just then I **stamp**ed my foot very hard.

"HEY! I WANT SOME ANSWERS DOWN HERE, HELEN! HE'S MY BABY TOO, YOU KNOW!"

Grandma Miller **frown**ed at me. 'Cause I'm not supposed to call her Helen, I think.

"Sorry," I said kind of quiet.

Then Grandma Miller **bend**ed down next to me. And so I didn't have to yell anymore.

"Are you telling me the truth, Grandma?" I said. "Is my brother *really* the cutest little monkey you ever saw? For really and **honest** and **truly**?"

Then my grandma Miller hugged me very tight.

"Yes, little girl," she **whisper**ed in my ear. "For really and honest and truly."

After that, she picked me up again. And me and her **twirl**ed all around the kitchen.

4
Hoppy and Russell

My room at **kindergarten** is named Room Nine.

I have two bestest[1] friends in that place. One of them has the name of Lucille.

Lucille sits right **exact**ly next to me.

She has a red chair. And also little red **fingernail**s which are very **glossy**.

---

1 **bestest** 단어 'best(최고의)'를 강조한 비격식적인 표현. '최고로 좋은'이라는 뜻을 나타내며, 어린아이가 주로 사용한다.

My other bestest friend is named Grace.

Me and that Grace sit together on the school bus. **Except** for not today we didn't. Because today Grampa Miller drove me.

Then he walked to Room Nine with me. And he **wave**d at my teacher.

Her name is Mrs.

She has another name, too. But I just like Mrs. and **that's all**.

When I first walked into my room, Lucille was looking at that Grace's **brand-new** shoes. And their name was pink high tops.[2]

"Hey, Grace! Those new shoes look very beautiful on you!" I said.

---

2 **high top** 하이 톱. 발목 부분이 길어 복사뼈까지 덮는 형태로 된 운동화.

But that **dumb** Grace didn't even say *thank you* to me.

"Grace is angry at you," said Lucille. "She said that she **rode** the bus today. And you weren't even there to save her a seat. And she had to sit next to an **icky** kid. Right, Grace?"

Grace **bob**bed her head up and down.

"Yes, only I couldn't help it, Grace," I said. "That's because I stayed at my grampa Miller's all night. And there's no bus at that place. And so he had to drive me here today."

Then I tried to hold that Grace's hand. Only she quick pulled it away.

"That's not very nice of you, Grace," I said. "And so guess what? Now I'm not going to tell you my special secret."

That's when that Grace called me a poopy head.[3]

Lucille held my hand. "*I* don't think you're a poopy head, Junie B.," she said. "And so you can tell me your special secret. And I won't tell anybody. Not even Grace."

That's when that Grace kicked Lucille in the leg.

And so Lucille pushed her down.

And Mrs. had to come pull them off each other.

I raised my hand very **polite**. "I wasn't **involve**d," I said to Mrs.

---

3 **poopy head** '멍청이', '바보'라는 뜻의 속어.

A B C D E

After that, we had to sit down and do some work. It was called **print**ing our numbers. Only I couldn't do mine that good. Because Lucille kept on talking to me, that's why.

"Come on, Junie B.," she said in her whispering voice. "Tell me your special secret. I won't tell. I promise."

"Yes, only I *can't*, Lucille," I said. "'Cause no talking to your **neighbor**, remember?"

Then Mrs. **snap**ped her fingers at me.

"SEE, LUCILLE? I TOLD YOU NO TALKING TO YOUR NEIGHBOR!" I **holler**ed. "NOW I GOT SNAPPED AT!"

Just then a boy named Jim said, "**Shush**," to me.

"Shush yourself, you big fat Jim," I said

back.

After that, Mrs. stood next to me till I finished my work. Then I got all done and she collected it.

That made me happy inside. Because guess what comes after work? Something very fun, that's what!

And its name is Show and Tell.[4]

Mrs. stood next to her desk. "Who has something interesting to share with the class today?" she said.

Then my heart got very **pumpy**. Because I had the most special secret in the whole wide world!

I raised my hand way high in the air.

---

4 **Show and Tell** 유치원이나 초등학교에서 자신에게 의미 있는 물건을 가지고 나와서 친구들과 선생님에게 설명하는 일종의 발표 시간.

"OOOOOH! OOOOOH!" I hollered real loud. "ME! ME! ME!"

Mrs. shook her head at me. Because I'**m** not **supposed to** go oooooh, oooooh, me, me, me.

She called on William. He is a **cry-baby** boy in my class. I can **beat** him up, I think.

"William?" said Mrs. "Since you raised your hand so politely, you may go first."

And so then William carried a paper bag to the front of the room. And he took out a **jar** of two dead **cricket**s.

Except for William didn't know they were dead. He just thought they were sleeping.

"Jump, Hoppy! Jump, Russell!" said

William.

Then he **tap**ped on the glass.

"Hey! Wake up in there!" he said.

After that, William started shaking the jar all over the place. And he wouldn't stop.

"WAKE UP, I SAID!" he shouted.

Then Hoppy and Russell started **fall**ing all **apart**. And Mrs. had to take the jar away.

That's when William started to cry. And he had to go to the nurse's office[5] to lie down.

And so then I raised my hand way high in the air again.

Because guess what? My Show and Tell was *way* better than two dead crickets!

---

5 **nurse's office** 보건실. 학교에서 학생이 아프거나 다쳤을 때를 대비하여 건강 및 위생 관리에 필요한 시설을 갖춘 곳.

5
Monkey Business

Mrs. called my name.

"Junie B.? Would you like to go next?" she asked.

Then I jumped right up. And I ran **speedy** fast to the front of the room.

"Guess what?" I said very excited. "Last night my mother had a baby! And it's the boy kind!"

Mrs. **clap**ped her hands.

"Junie B. Jones has a new little brother, everyone!" she said. "Isn't that wonderful?"

Then all of Room Nine clapped, too.

"Yes, only you haven't even heard the bestest part yet!" I said very loud. "Because guess what else? He's a MONKEY! That's what else! My new brother is a real, alive, baby MONKEY!!!"

Mrs. got a funny look on her face. And she **squint**ed her eyes very **tiny**. And so maybe she didn't hear me or something, I think.

"I SAID I'VE GOT A MONKEY BROTHER!" I shouted real louder.

Then that **mean** Jim jumped right up from his desk. And he hollered, "Liar, liar, pants on fire![1]”

“No they are not on fire, you big fat Jim!” I said back. “I do too have a monkey brother! You can ask my grandma Miller

1 **liar, liar, pants on fire** 거짓말을 한 사람을 장난스럽게 놀리는 말로, ‘liar’와 ‘fire’의 라임이 노래처럼 리듬감을 형성한다.

if you don't believe me!"

Mrs. raised her **eyebrows** way high on her head.

"Your grandmother told you that your brother is a monkey?" she asked me.

"Yes!" I said. "She told me he has long

fingers and long **toe**s. And lots of black **fur** all over himself!"

After that, Mrs. kept on looking and looking at me. Then she said it was time for me to sit down.

"Yeah, only I'm not done telling the children about my monkey brother yet," I explained.

"'Cause guess what else? His **wallpaper** has pictures of his **jungle** friends on it. And his bed has **bar**s on the sides. But I'm going to teach him not to **bite** or kill people."

Then this boy named Ricardo—who has cute **freckle**s on his face—said, "Monkeys are cool," to me.

"I know they are cool, Ricardo," I said.

"And guess what else? Maybe I can bring him to school on **Pet** Day."

Then Ricardo smiled at me. And so he might be my boyfriend, I think. Except for there's a boy in Room Eight who already loves me.

Just then, Mrs. stood up and pointed at me.

"That's *enough,* Junie B.," she said. "I want you to sit down now. You and I will talk about this monkey business later."

And so that made me **giggle**. Because monkey business is a funny word, I think.

Then I **wave**d good-bye to my new boyfriend, Ricardo.

And I **skip**ped back to my seat.

6
Bestest Friends

Recess is my best **subject**. I learned it my first week at school.

Recess is when you go outside. And you run off your **steam**.

Then when you come in, you can sit still better. And you don't have ants in your pants.[1]

1 **have ants in one's pants** '초조해하다', '안절부절못하다'라는 뜻의 숙어.

At recess, me and Lucille and that Grace play horses together.

I'm Brownie. Lucille is Blackie. And that Grace is Yellowie.

"I'M BROWNIE!" I **holler**ed as soon as I got outside.

"I don't want to play horses today," said Lucille. "I want to know some more about your monkey brother."

"Me, too," said that Grace.

Then Lucille pushed that Grace out of the way. And she **whisper**ed a secret in my ear.

"If you let me be the first one to see him, I'll let you wear my new locket,[2]"

---

2 **locket** 로켓. 작은 사진이나 기념할 만한 것을 넣는 펜던트나 그 펜던트가 달린 목걸이.

she said.

"Yeah. Only guess what, Lucille?" I said. "I don't even know what a **dumb** locket is."

And so then Lucille showed me her locket. It was a little gold heart on a **chain**.

"Isn't it **beauteous**?" she said. "My **nanna** gave it to me for my birthday."

Then she opened up the little heart. And there was a little **bitty** picture inside of that thing!

"Hey! There's a **teeny** head in there!" I said very excited.

"I know," said Lucille. "That's my nanna. See her?"

I **squint**ed very hard at the little

picture.

"Your nanna is a shrimpie,[3] Lucille," I said.

After that, Lucille closed the locket. And she gave it to me.

"Now I'm your best friend, right, Junie B.?" she said. "And so I can be the first one to see your monkey brother!"

Just then, that Grace **stomp**ed her foot very hard.

"No you cannot, Lucille!" she hollered. "*I'm* her best friend! 'Cause me and her **ride** the bus together. And so I get to see her monkey brother first. Right, Junie B.? Right? Right?"

---

3 **shrimpie** '아주 작은 사람'을 뜻하는 속어 'shrimp'를 주니 B.가 'shrimpie'라고 장난스럽게 말한 표현.

I made my **shoulder**s go up and down.

"I don't know, Grace," I said. "'Cause Lucille just gave me this locket with the teeny nanna. And so that means she gets to go first, I think."

That Grace stomped her foot again. She **made a** mad **face** at me.

"Pooey![4]" she said.

Except for just then I got a great idea!

"Hey! Guess what, Grace?" I said very excited. "Since Lucille gave me something beautiful, now you can give me something beautiful, too! And so that would be very **fair** of me, I think!"

Then that Grace started smiling. And

---

4 **pooey** '이런' 또는 '젠장'의 의미로 혐오, 경멸, 짜증 등을 나타내는 속어적 표현.

she **took off** her **sparkly** new ring.

"Here!" she said. "I got it out of cereal this morning! See how **shiny** the stone is? That's because it's a real **genuine fake** plastic diamond."

Then she put some breath on it. And she shined it on her **sleeve** for me.

"Oooooh," I said. "I love this thing, Grace."

"I know," she said. "And so now I get to see your monkey brother first. Right, Junie B.? Right?"

After that I had to think a little bit.

"Yeah, only here's the trouble, Grace," I said. "Now I have one thing from you and one thing from Lucille. And so it's a **tie**."

Then Lucille quick took off her red

sweater with the Scottie dog[5] on it. And she tied it around my **waist**.

"Here!" she said. "Now I've given you two things! And so I'm still the winner."

"Oh no you're not!" hollered that Grace. "Because I'm gonna give Junie B. my **snack** ticket for today. And so she can have my cookie and milk!"

"Excellent idea, Grace!" I said.

Then me and her did a **high five**.

"Oh yeah?" said Lucille. "Well, then I'm going to give her *my* snack ticket, too! And so I'm still the winner!"

After that Grace looked all over herself.

---

5 **Scottie dog** 개의 한 품종인 '스코티시테리어(Scottish terrier)'의 애칭. 작은 체구와 뾰족한 귀, 그리고 위로 올라간 꼬리가 특징이다.

“But that’s not fair,” she said. "Because I don’t have anything else to give her.”

And so I looked all over her, too. And

then I jumped up and down again.

"Yes you do, Grace!" I said. "You do too have something else to give me! And their name is your new pink high tops!"

That Grace **stare**d at her feet. She looked very sad.

"Yeah, only this is the first time I ever wore these," she said real quiet.

And so I **pat**ted her so she would feel better.

"I know, Grace," I explained nicely. "But if you don't give them to me, then you won't be able to see my monkey brother."

And so then me and that Grace sat down on the grass. And she took off her new pink shoes. And she gave them to me.

"Thank you, Grace," I said **polite**ly.

Then I stood up.

"Okay. Your **turn**," I said to Lucille.

Only too bad for me. 'Cause just then the stupid bell rang.

7
Some School Words

I wore my **brand-new** things back to Room Nine.

They looked very beautiful on me. Except my new pink high tops were too big. And my feet were very **sliding** around in there.

Before I sat down I looked at Lucille's red chair. Then I **tap**ped on her.

"I'm sorry, Lucille," I said. "But red is

my favorite color. And so I would like that chair of yours, I think."

Lucille looked very **upset** at me. "But red is my favorite color, too, Junie B."

I **pat**ted her. "I know, Lucille," I said nicely. "But you still must give it to me. It's the **rule**s."

And so she did.

"Now I'm the winner for sure, aren't I?" she asked.

I made my **shoulder**s go up and down. "I don't know, Lucille," I said. "That Grace said she might have some **cash** in her **purse**."

After that, Mrs. passed out construction paper.[1] And we cut out autumn leaves for our **bulletin board**.

Autumn is the school word for fall.

We **sprinkle**d our leaves with **shiny glitter**.

Also, I sprinkled glitter in my hair. And I **paste**d some to my **eyebrow**s.

Then Mrs. **confiscate**d my shiny glitter **jar**.

Confiscate is the school word for **yank**ed it right out of my hand.

Just then, Mrs. Gutzman **knock**ed on our door. And she came into the room with our milk and cookies.

"**HURRAY**! HURRAY FOR MRS. GUTZMAN!" I shouted at her. "GUESS WHAT, MRS. GUTZMAN? I GET THREE

1 **construction paper** 색지. 여러 가지 색깔로 물들인 종이로 주로 어린 아이들이 공작 활동을 할 때 사용한다.

SNACKS TODAY! SEE? I HAVE THREE SNACK TICKETS!"

Mrs. walked over to my chair. She **stare**d down at me.

"How did you get two **extra** tickets, Junie B.?" she asked. "Did you find them on the **playground**?"

Then she took my two extra tickets away. And she held them way high in the air.

"Did anyone lose their snack tickets today?" she said to the class.

"NO!" I hollered. "Those are my tickets! Lucille and Grace gave them to me!"

Mrs. raised her eyebrows. "Lucille? Did you give Junie B. your snack ticket today?" she asked.

"Yes," said Lucille. "That's because she made me."

"No, I did not, you dumb Lucille!" I said. "I did not make you!"

Mrs. said, "Be quiet," to me.

She **fold**ed her arms. "Grace? Did you give your snack ticket to Junie B., too?"

Then that Grace started to cry. Because she thought she was in trouble.

Mrs. tapped her foot. "Please come get your snack ticket, Grace," she said.

And so then that Grace walked to my table in just her socks.

And Mrs. made **squinty** eyes at her feet.

"Where are your shoes, Grace?" she asked.

COOKIES

That's when big fat baby Grace started crying very harder. And she pointed at her shoes.

Mrs. **peep**ed under my table.

"Junie B. Jones!" she hollered. "Why are you wearing Grace's shoes?"

Mrs. sounded dangerous.

"Because," I said kind of **scare**d.

"Because why?" said Mrs.

"Because it's the rules," I explained.

Then Mrs. **bend**ed down very close to my ear. "What rules?"

"The rules for who gets to be the first one to see my monkey brother," I said.

Mrs. **roll**ed **her eyes** way back in her head.

"Put your own shoes back on. And

come with me, young lady," she said.

Then me and her walked into the **hall** together. And she made me tell her what happened on the playground.

After that, I had to give Lucille back the locket and the sweater with the Scottie dog on it. And I had to give Grace back the real **genuine fake** ring from cereal.

Then Mrs. wrote a note. And she said for me to take it to the office.

The office is where the **boss** of the school lives. His name is **Principal**.

"Yes, but I don't think I would like to go down there today," I said. "Or else my mother might get mad at me."

Mrs. tapped her foot. Then she took hold of my hand.

"Let's go, young lady. **March,**" she said.

And so then me and her marched to the office.

March is the school word for pulled me way too fast.

8
Me and Principal

The school office is a **scary** place.

It has loud ringing phones. And a **typing** lady who is a stranger. And a **row** of chairs where bad kids sit.

Mrs. **plop**ped me in a blue one.

"Wait here," she said.

"Yeah, only I'm not bad," I **whisper**ed to just myself.

Then I put my sweater on my head. So

PRINCIPA

nobody would see me in the bad kid's chair.

After that, I **peek**ed down my long sweater **sleeve**. And I saw Mrs. out of my hand hole. She was **knock**ing on Principal's door.

Then she went in there. And my heart felt very **pump**y. Because she was **tattletaling**[1] on me, I think.

After a while, she came out again.

Principal came with her.

Principal has a **baldy** head which looks like **rubber**.

Also, he has big hands. And heavy

---

1 **tattletale** 주로 명사 또는 형용사로 쓰이는 단어 'tattletale(고자질쟁이, 고자질하는)'을 여기에서는 '고자질하다'라는 의미의 동사처럼 사용했다.

shoes. And a suit made out of black.

"Could I see you in my office for a minute, Junie B.?" he said.

And so then I had to go in there all **by myself**. And I sat in a big wood chair. And Principal made me **take** the sweater **off** my head.

"So what's this all about?" he said. "Why do you think your teacher brought you down here today?"

"Because," I said very quiet.

"Because why?" said Principal.

"Because that Grace **shot off her** big fat **mouth**," I explained.

Then Principal **fold**ed his arms. And he said for me to start at the beginning.

And so I did. . . .

First, I told him about how I spended the night at my grampa's house.

"We had delicious waffles for breakfast," I said. "And I had five of them. Only my grampa didn't know where I put them all. **Except** I put them way in here."

Then I opened my mouth and showed Principal where my waffles went.

After that, I told him how my grandma Miller came home from the hospital. And she told me I had a monkey brother. For really and **honest** and **truly**.

"And so then I told the children at Show and Tell," I said. "And at **recess** Lucille and that Grace started giving me lots of pretty **stuff**. Because they wanted to be first to see him.

"Except too bad for me," I said. "Because when we came inside, Mrs. found out about the **snack** tickets. And then that **dumb** Grace shot off her big fat mouth about her shoes. And so I got **march**ed down here. And I had to sit in the bad kid's chair."

Then I **smooth**ed my skirt. "The end," I said nicely.

Principal **rub**bed his head that looks like rubber.

"Junie B., maybe we should go back to when your grandmother came home from the hospital," he said. "Can you remember *exactly* what she said about your brother being a monkey?"

I **scrunch**ed my eyes real tight to

remember.

"Yes," I said. "Grandma Miller said he was the cutest little monkey she ever saw."

Then Principal closed his eyes. "Aaah," he said kind of quiet. "Now I get it."

After that, he smiled a little bit. "You see, Junie B., when your grandmother called your brother a little monkey, she didn't mean he was a *real* little monkey. She just meant he was, well . . . cute."

"I know he's cute," I said. "That's because all monkeys are cute. Except for I don't like the big kind that can kill you."

Principal shook his head. "No, Junie B., that's not what I mean. I mean your brother isn't really a monkey at all. He's just a little baby boy."

I made a **frowny** face. "No, he is *not* a little baby boy," I told him. "He's a real, alive, baby monkey with black **hairy fur** and long fingers and **toes**. You can ask my grandma Miller if you don't believe me."

And so guess what Principal did then? He called her, that's what! He called Grandma Miller right up on the phone!

And then he talked to her. And then I talked to her too!

"Hey, Grandma!" I said very shouty. "Guess what just happened down here? Principal said that my baby brother isn't a real, alive monkey. Only he is. 'Cause you told me that. Remember? You said he was a monkey. For really and honest and truly."

Then Grandma Miller said she was very sorry. But she didn't mean he was a *real* monkey. She just meant he was *cute*.

Just like Principal explained to me.

And so then I felt very **droopy** inside.

"Yeah, only what about all of his black hair? And his long fingers and toes?" I said. "And what about his bed that looks like a **cage**? And the **wallpaper** with his **jungle** friends on it?"

But Grandma Miller kept on saying that my new brother was just a **regular** cute baby. And so finally I didn't want to talk to her anymore. And I **hang**ed **up** the phone.

Then I **bend**ed my head way down.

And my eyes got a little bit of wet in them.

"Darn it," I said very quiet.

After that, Principal gave me a **tissue**. And he said, "I'm sorry," to me.

Then he held my hand.

And me and him walked back to Room Nine.

9
Pigs and Ducks and Stuff

Principal went into Room Nine with me.

Then he **clap**ped his **giant** hands together.

"Boys and girls? May I please have your **attention**?" he said. "I would like to explain what happened during Show and Tell today. It's about Junie B. Jones and her new baby brother."

Just then that Jim I hate jumped right

up out of his chair.

"He's not a monkey, is he?" he shouted very loud. "I knew it! I knew he wasn't a monkey!"

I made a big **fist** at him. "HOW WOULD YOU LIKE THIS UP YOUR NOSE, YOU BIG **DUMB** JIM?" I **holler**ed.

Then Principal **frown**ed at me. And so I smiled.

"I hate that guy," I said nicely.

After that, Principal took a big breath.

"Boys and girls, there's a good reason why Junie B. told you that her baby brother was a monkey," he said.

"Yeah! It was all my grandma Miller's **fault**!" I **interrupt**ed. "Because she told me that my brother was a *little monkey.*

Only she didn't mean he was a *real* little monkey. She just meant he was cute. Only who the heck[1] knew that dumb thing?"

Principal made another frown at me. Then he talked some more.

"You see, boys and girls," he said. "Sometimes adults say things that can be very **confusing** to children. Like what if you heard me talking about a *lucky duck?*[2] You might think I was talking about a **real live** duck. But *lucky duck* just means a lucky person."

"Right," said Mrs. "And when we call someone a *busy bee,*[3] we don't mean

---

1 **heck** '도대체', '젠장' 또는 '제기랄'이라는 뜻으로 당혹스럽거나 짜증스러운 감정을 강조하는 속어.

2 **lucky duck** 굉장히 운이 좋은 사람을 이르는 말.

3 **busy bee** 일벌레. 부지런히 일하는 사람을 이르는 말.

he's a real bee. We just mean he's a hard worker."

"Hey! I just thought of another one!" I said very excited. "A dumb bunny isn't a real alive bunny, either! It's just a **plain** old dumb guy!"

Then my friend Lucille raised her hand.

"I've got one, too," she said. "Sometimes my **nanna** calls my daddy a **couch** potato.[4] Only he's not a real potato. He's just a lazy **bum**."

"Yeah, and I'm not a big pig," said my new boyfriend Ricardo. "But my mom says I eat like one."

After that, a whole **bunch** of other kids

---

4 **couch potato** 하루 종일 소파에 앉아 텔레비전만 보며 시간을 보내는 게으른 사람을 이르는 말.

said they eat like big pigs, too.

Only a boy named Donald said he eats like a horse.[5]

And **cry-baby** William eats like a bird.[6]

Just then it was time for the bell to ring. And so me and Principal said bye-bye to each other. And I went to my seat.

Then I gave Lucille back her red chair. She was very nice to me.

"I'm sorry that your brother isn't a real monkey, Junie B.," she said.

"Thank you, Lucille," I said. "I'm sorry that your daddy isn't a real potato, too."

After that, the bell rang for us to go home. And so me and Lucille and that

---

5 **eat like a horse** '아주 많이 먹다'라는 뜻의 숙어.

6 **eat like a bird** '새 모이 먹듯 먹다', '아주 적게 먹다'라는 뜻의 숙어.

Grace held hands. And we walked outside together.

Only then a very wonderful thing happened!

And it's called—I heard my mother's voice!

"JUNIE B.! JUNIE B.! OVER HERE, HONEY. DADDY AND I ARE OVER HERE!"

Then I looked in the **parking lot**. And I saw her! And so I runned to her **speedy** quick. And then me and Mother **hug**ged and hugged. Because I hadn't seen her for a very whole day!

Then my daddy got out of the car. And he had a little yellow **blanket** in his arms. And guess what was in that thing?

My new baby brother, that's what!

He was very **teeny**. And **pinkish**. **Except** his head had a lot of black hair on it.

I touched it. It felt like **fuzzy**.

Just then Ricardo walked by. And he saw my teeny brother.

"Cool hair," he said.

I smiled very big. "I know it, Ricardo," I said. "And guess what else? He doesn't even smell like P.U."

After that I got in the car. And I told Mother about Lucille's locket. And she said maybe I could get a locket, too. And I could put my brother's teeny head in there.

"Yes. And I would also like some pink

high tops, please," I said very **polite**.

"Maybe," said Mother.

"Oh boy![8]" I said.

---

8 **boy** 여기에서는 '소년'이라는 뜻이 아니라, '맙소사' 또는 '어머나'라는 의미로 놀람이나 기쁨 등을 나타내는 표현으로 쓰였다.

'Cause *maybe* doesn't mean no! That's why!

And so then I **lift**ed up the blanket. And I **peep**ed at my baby brother one more time.

"So what do you think of him, Junie B.?" said Mother.

I smiled very big. "I think he's the cutest little monkey I ever saw," I said.

Then Mother laughed.

And I laughed, too.

junie b. jones series

1 Junie B. Jones and the Stupid Smelly Bus
2 Junie B. Jones and a Little Monkey Business
3 Junie B. Jones and Her Big Fat Mouth
4 Junie B. Jones and Some Sneaky Peeky Spying
5 Junie B. Jones and the Yucky Blucky Fruitcake
6 Junie B. Jones and That Meanie Jim's Birthday
7 Junie B. Jones Loves Handsome Warren
8 Junie B. Jones Has a Monster Under Her Bed
9 Junie B. Jones Is Not a Crook
10 Junie B. Jones Is a Party Animal

It's pooey on B-A-B-I-E-S until . . .

Junie B. Jones finds out that her new baby brother is a big fat deal. Her two bestest friends are giving her everything they own just to see him. And guess what else? Maybe she can bring him to school on Pet Day.

"Junie B. is the darling of the young-reader set."
—*USA Today*

9 791191 343090 14740
ISBN 979-11-91343-09-0

junie b. jones®

주니 B. 존스와 아기 원숭이 소동

by BARBARA PARK

illustrated by
Denise Brunkus

롱테일북스

CONTENTS

세상에서 가장 엉뚱하고 재미있는 아이, 주니 B. 존스의 좌충우돌 성장기!

『주니 B. 존스(Junie B. Jones)』 시리즈는 호기심 많은 개구쟁이 소녀 주니 B.가 일상에서 마주하는 다양한 상황을 재치 있게 담고 있습니다. 주니 B.는 언제나 자신의 감정을 솔직하게 표현하며, 재미있는 생각이 떠오르면 주저없이 실행에 옮기는 적극적인 여섯 살 소녀입니다. 이렇게 유쾌하고 재기 발랄한 주니 B. 존스의 성장기는 지금까지 전 세계적으로 6천 5백만 부 이상 판매되며 수많은 독자들에게 사랑받았고, 연극과 뮤지컬로 제작되기도 했습니다.

저자 바바라 파크(Barbara Park)는 첫 등교, 친구 관계, 동생에 대한 고민 등과 같이 일상 속 다양한 상황에서 아이들이 느끼는 감정을 그들의 시선으로 탁월하게 묘사했습니다. 특히 아이들이 영어로 말할 때 저지르기 쉬운 실수도 자연스럽게 녹여 내어, 이야기에 더욱 공감하게 합니다.

이러한 이유로 『주니 B. 존스』 시리즈는 '엄마표 영어'를 진행하는 부모님과 초보 영어 학습자에게 반드시 읽어야 할 영어원서로 자리 잡았습니다. 친근한 어휘와 쉬운 문장으로 쓰여 있어 더욱 몰입하여 읽을 수 있는 『주니 B. 존스』 시리즈는 영어원서가 친숙하지 않은 학습자들에게도 즐거운 원서 읽기 경험을 선사할 것입니다.

퀴즈와 단어장, 그리고 번역까지 담긴 알찬 구성의 워크북!

이 책은 영어원서 『주니 B. 존스』 시리즈에, 탁월한 학습 효과를 거둘 수 있도록 다양한 콘텐츠를 덧붙인 책입니다.

- 영어원서: 본문에 나온 어려운 어휘에 볼드 처리가 되어 있어 단어를 더욱 분명히 인지하며 자연스럽게 암기하게 됩니다.
- 단어장: 원서에 나온 어려운 어휘가 '한영'은 물론 '영영' 의미까지 완벽하게 정리되어 있으며, 반복되는 단어까지 표시하여 자연스럽게 복습이 되도록 구성했습니다.
- 번역: 영어와 비교할 수 있도록 직역에 가까운 번역을 담았습니다. 원서 읽기에 익숙하지 않은 초보 학습자도 어려움 없이 내용을 파악할 수 있습니다.
- 퀴즈: 챕터별로 내용을 확인하는 이해력 점검 퀴즈가 들어 있습니다.

『주니 B. 존스』, 이렇게 읽어 보세요!

- **단어 암기는 이렇게!** 처음 리딩을 시작하기 전, 해당 챕터에 나오는 단어를 눈으로 쭉 훑어봅니다. 모르는 단어는 좀 더 주의 깊게 보되, 손으로 쓰면서 완벽하게 암기할 필요는 없습니다. 본문을 읽으면서 이 단어를 다시 만나게 되는데, 그 과정에서 단어의 쓰임새와 어감을 자연스럽게 익히게 됩니다. 이렇게 책을 읽은 후에, 단어를 다시 한번 복습하세요. 복습할 때는 중요하다고 생각하는 단어들을 손으로 쓰면서 꼼꼼하게 외우는 것도 좋습니다. 이런 방식으로 책을 읽다 보면, 많은 단어를 빠르고 부담 없이 익히게 됩니다.

- **리딩할 때는 리딩에만 집중하자!** 원서를 읽는 중간중간 모르는 단어가 나온다고 워크북을 들춰 보거나, 곧바로 번역을 찾아보는 것은 매우 좋지 않은 습관입니다. 모르는 단어나 이해가 가지 않는 문장이 나온다고 해도 펜으로 가볍게 표시만 해 두고, 전체적인 맥락을 잡아 가며 빠르게 읽어 나가세요. 리딩을 할 때는 속도에 대한 긴장감을 잃지 않으면서 리딩에만 집중하는 것이 좋습니다. 모르는 단어와 문장은, 리딩이 끝난 후에 한꺼번에 정리하는 '리뷰' 시간을 통해 점검합니다. 리뷰를 할 때는 번역은 물론 단어장과 사전도 꼼꼼하게 확인하면서 왜 이해가 되지 않았는지 확인해 봅니다.

- **번역 활용은 이렇게!** 이해가 가지 않는 문장은 번역을 통해서 그 의미를 파악할 수 있습니다. 하지만 한국어와 영어는 정확히 1:1 대응이 되지 않기 때문에 번역을 활용하는 데에도 지혜가 필요합니다. 의역이 된 부분까지 억지로 의미를 대응해서 암기하려고 하기보다, 어떻게 그런 의미가 만들어진 것인지 추측하면서 번역은 참고 자료로 활용하는 것이 좋습니다.

- **2~3번 반복해서 읽자!** 영어 초보자라면 2~3회 반복해서 읽을 것을 추천합니다. 초보자일수록 처음 읽을 때는 생소한 단어와 스토리 때문에 내용 파악에 급급할 수밖에 없습니다. 하지만 일단 내용을 파악한 후에 다시 읽으면 어휘와 문장 구조 등 다른 부분까지 관찰하면서 조금 더 깊이 있게 읽을 수 있고, 그 과정에서 리딩 속도도 빨라지고 리딩 실력을 더 확고하게 다지게 됩니다.

- **'시리즈'로 꾸준히 읽자!** 한 작가의 책을 시리즈로 읽는 것 또한 영어 실력 향상에 큰 도움이 됩니다. 같은 등장인물이 다시 나오기 때문에 내용 파악이 더 수월할 뿐 아니라, 작가가 사용하는 어휘와 표현들도 자연스럽게 반복되기 때문에 탁월한 복습 효과까지 얻을 수 있습니다. 『주니 B. 존스』 시리즈는 현재 3권, 총 18,819단어 분량이 출간되어 있습니다. 시리즈를 꾸준히 읽다 보면 영어 실력도 자연스럽게 향상될 것입니다.

영어원서 본문 구성

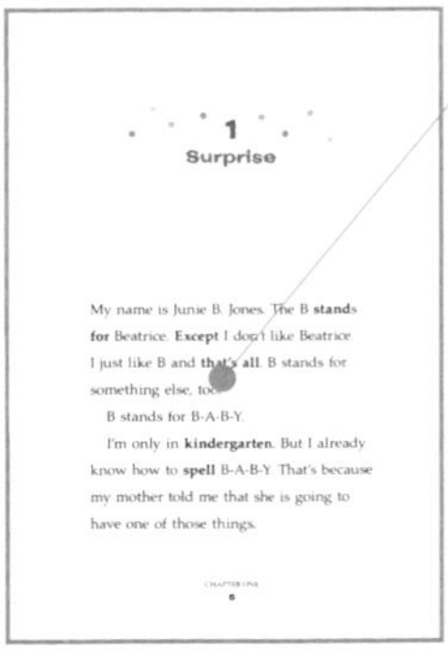

1
Surprise

My name is Junie B. Jones. The B **stands for** Beatrice. **Except** I don't like Beatrice. I just like B and **that's all**. B stands for something else, too.

B stands for B-A-B-Y.

I'm only in **kindergarten**. But I already know how to **spell** B-A-B-Y. That's because my mother told me that she is going to have one of those things.

CHAPTER ONE

내용이 담긴 본문입니다.

원어민이 읽는 일반 원서와 같은 텍스트지만, 암기해야 할 중요 어휘는 볼드체로 표시되어 있습니다. 이 어휘들은 지금 들고 계신 워크북에 챕터별로 정리되어 있습니다.

학습 심리학 연구 결과에 따르면, 한 단어씩 따로 외우는 단어 암기는 거의 효과가 없다고 합니다. 대신 단어를 제대로 외우기 위해서는 문맥(Context) 속에서 단어를 암기해야 하며, 한 단어 당 문맥 속에서 15번 이상 마주칠 때 완벽하게 암기할 수 있다고 합니다.

이 책의 본문은 중요 어휘를 볼드로 강조하여, 문맥 속의 단어들을 더 확실히 인지(Word Cognition in Context)하도록 돕고 있습니다. 또한 대부분의 중요한 단어는 다른 챕터에서도 반복해서 등장하기 때문에 이 책을 읽는 것만으로도 자연스럽게 어휘력을 향상시킬 수 있습니다.

또한 본문에는 내용 이해를 돕기 위해 '각주'가 첨가되어 있습니다. 각주는 굳이 암기할 필요는 없지만, 알아 두면 내용을 더 깊이 있게 이해할 수 있어 원서를 읽는 재미가 배가됩니다.

Mother made me sit up. Then she and my daddy said some more **stuff** about a baby.

"The baby will be yours, too, Junie B.," Daddy said. "Just think. You'll have your very own little brother or sister to play with. Won't that be fun?"

I did my **shoulder**s up and down again. "I don't know. Maybe," I said.

Then I got down from my chair and ran into the living room.

"BAD NEWS, **FELLAS**!" I **holler**ed very loud. "THE PRESENT ISN'T IN THIS **DUMB** BUNNY[4] ROOM, EITHER!"

Mother and Daddy came into the

CHAPTER ONE

워크북(Workbook)의 구성

Check Your Reading Speed

해당 챕터의 단어 수가 기록되어 있어, 리딩 속도를 측정할 수 있습니다. 특히 리딩 속도를 중시하는 독자는 유용하게 사용할 수 있습니다.

Build Your Vocabulary

본문에 볼드 표시되어 있는 단어가 정리되어 있습니다. 리딩 전, 후에 반복해서 보면 원서를 더욱 쉽게 읽을 수 있고, 어휘력도 빠르게 향상됩니다.

단어는 〈빈도 – 스펠링 – 발음기호 – 품사 – 한국어 뜻 – 영어 뜻〉 순서로 표기되어 있으며 빈도 표시(★)가 많을수록 필수 어휘입니다. 반복해서 등장하는 단어는 빈도 대신 '복습'으로 표기되어 있습니다. 품사는 아래와 같이 표기했습니다.

n. **명사** | a. **형용사** | ad. **부사** | v. **동사**
conj. **접속사** | prep. **전치사** | int. **감탄사** | idiom **숙어 및 관용구**

Comprehension Quiz

간단한 퀴즈를 통해 읽은 내용에 대한 이해력을 점검해 볼 수 있습니다.

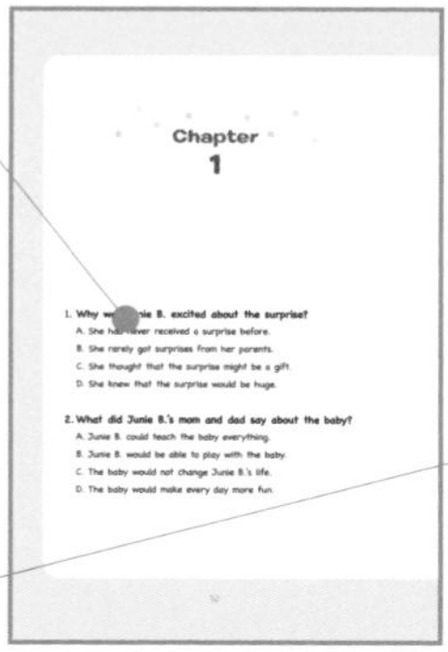

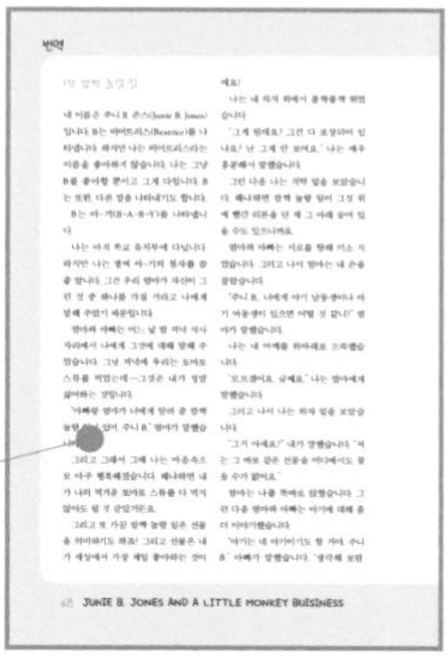

번역

영문과 비교할 수 있도록 최대한 직역에 가까운 번역을 담았습니다.

이 책의 수준과 타깃 독자

- **미국 원어민 기준**: 유치원 ~ 초등학교 저학년
- **한국 학습자 기준**: 초등학교 저학년 ~ 중학생
- **영어원서 완독 경험이 없는 초보 영어 학습자** (토익 기준 450~750점대)
- **비슷한 수준의 다른 챕터북**: Arthur Chapter Book, Flat Stanley, The Zack Files, Magic Tree House, Marvin Redpost
- **도서 분량**: 약 6,000단어

아이도 어른도 재미있게 읽는 영어원서를
〈롱테일 에디션〉으로 만나 보세요!

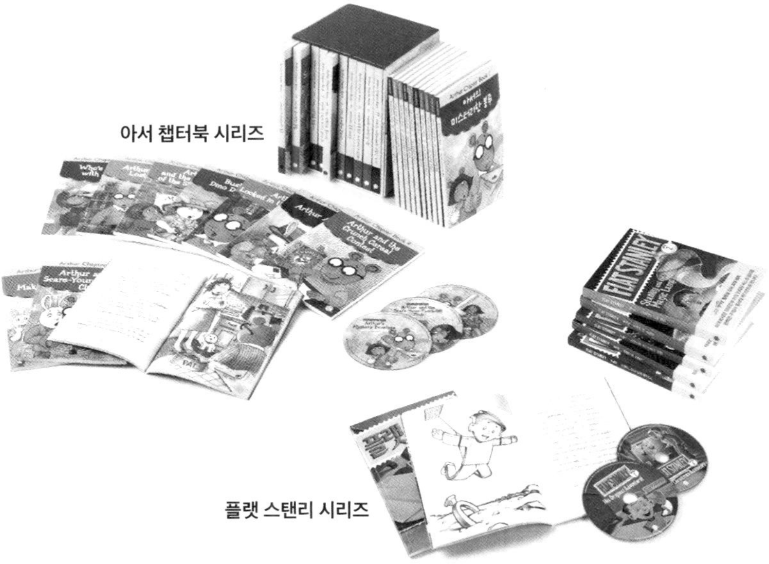

Chapter 1

1. Why was Junie B. excited about the surprise?

A. She had never received a surprise before.

B. She rarely got surprises from her parents.

C. She thought that the surprise might be a gift.

D. She knew that the surprise would be huge.

2. What did Junie B.'s mom and dad say about the baby?

A. Junie B. could teach the baby everything.

B. Junie B. would be able to play with the baby.

C. The baby would not change Junie B.'s life.

D. The baby would make every day more fun.

3. How did Junie B. react to her mom and dad's news?

A. She thought that it was a joke.

B. She was thrilled about it.

C. She was totally shocked by it.

D. She was not satisfied with it.

4. What did Junie B. think that her mom should do?

A. Say sorry for the bad surprise

B. Remind Junie B. that she loved her

C. Explain why having a baby was a good thing

D. Buy a big present for Junie B.

5. What would Junie B.'s mom do if the baby smelled bad?

A. Make the baby leave the room

B. Let Junie B. spray an air freshener

C. Open all the windows in the house

D. Get some fresh flowers

Check Your Reading Speed

1분에 몇 단어를 읽는지 리딩 속도를 측정해 보세요.

$$\frac{649 \text{ words}}{\text{reading time (} \qquad \text{) sec}} \times 60 = (\qquad) \text{ WPM}$$

Build Your Vocabulary

stand for idiom 나타내다; 옹호하다
If one or more letters stand for a word or name, they are the first letter or letters of that word or name and they represent it.

★★ **except** [iksépt] conj. ~이지만, ~라는 점만 제외하면; prep. ~ 외에는; v. 제외하다
You can use except to introduce a statement that makes what you have just said seem less true or less possible.

that's all idiom 그게 다이다, 그뿐이다
You can say 'that's all' at the end of a sentence when you say that there is nothing more involved than what you have mentioned.

kindergarten [kíndərgà:rtn] n. 유치원
A kindergarten is a school or class for children aged 4 to 6 years old. It prepares them to go into the first grade.

★★ **spell** [spel] v. (어떤 단어의) 철자를 쓰다; 철자를 맞게 쓰다; n. 주문, 마법
When you spell a word, you write or speak each letter in the word in the correct order.

★ **stew** [stju:] v. (음식을) 뭉근히 끓이다; n. 스튜 (**stewed** a. 뭉근히 끓인)
Stewed fruit or meat has been cooked slowly in a liquid.

★ **bounce** [bauns] v. 깡충깡충 뛰다; 튀다; n. 튐, 튀어 오름; 탄력
If you bounce on a soft surface, you jump up and down on it repeatedly.

wrap [ræp] v. 포장하다; 둘러싸다; (무엇의 둘레를) 두르다; n. 포장지; 랩
When you wrap something, you fold paper or cloth tightly around it to cover it completely, for example when you are giving it as a present.

silly [síli] a. 어리석은, 바보 같은; 우스꽝스러운; n. 바보
If you say that someone or something is silly, you mean that they are foolish, childish, or ridiculous.

stuff [stʌf] n. 것, 물건, 일; v. 채워 넣다; 쑤셔 넣다
You can use stuff to refer to things such as a substance, a collection of things, events, or ideas, or the contents of something in a general way without mentioning the thing itself by name.

shoulder [ʃóuldər] n. 어깨; (옷의) 어깨 부분
Your shoulder is one of the two parts of your body between your neck and the top of your arms.

fella [félə] n. (pl.) 여러분, 얘들아; 남자; 남자 친구
You can use fellas as a term of address when you are talking to several people.

holler [hálər] v. 소리 지르다, 고함치다; n. 고함, 외침
If you holler, you shout loudly.

dumb [dʌm] a. 멍청한, 바보 같은; 말을 못하는
If you say that something is dumb, you think that it is silly and annoying.

smiley [smáili] a. 상냥한, 웃는 얼굴의; n. 미소 표시
If someone is smiley, they look friendly and smile a lot.

fold [fould] v. (두 손·팔 등을) 끼다; 접다, 접히다; n. 주름; 접힌 부분
(fold one's arms idiom 팔짱을 끼다)
If you fold your arms or hands, you bring them together and cross or link them, for example, over your chest.

make a face idiom 얼굴을 일그러뜨리다
If you make a face, you show a feeling such as dislike or disgust by putting an exaggerated expression on your face.

grumpy [grʌ́mpi] a. 심술이 난, 기분이 언짢은; 성격이 나쁜
If you say that someone is grumpy, you mean that they are bad-tempered and miserable.

all of a sudden idiom 갑자기
If something happens all of a sudden, it happens quickly and unexpectedly.

growly [gráuli] a. 으르렁거리는; 화를 잘 내는
If you make a growly sound, you make a low noise in your throat, usually because you are angry.

give up idiom 그만두다; 포기하다; 단념하다
If you give up, you decide that you cannot do something and stop trying to do it.

⁑ **owe** [ou] v. (감사 등을) 나타낼 의무가 있다; 신세를 지다, ~해야 한다; (돈을) 빚지고 있다
If you say that you owe someone gratitude, respect, or loyalty, you mean that they deserve it from you.

⋆ **apology** [əpálədʒi] n. 사죄, 사과
An apology is something that you say or write in order to tell someone that you are sorry that you have hurt them or caused trouble for them.

wrinkly [ríŋkli] a. 주름진, 주름이 있는
When you make a wrinkly nose or a wrinkly forehead, you tighten the muscles in your face so that the skin folds.

spit-up [spít-ʌp] n. 토
Spit-up is stomach contents such as milk which are vomited, especially by a child.

stink [stiŋk] n. 악취; v. (고약한) 냄새가 나다, 악취가 풍기다; 수상쩍다
Stink means a strong unpleasant smell.

⁑ **bomb** [bam] n. 폭탄; v. 폭탄으로 공격하다, 폭격하다
A bomb is a device which explodes and damages or destroys a large area.

air freshener [έər frèʃənər] n. 방향제
An air freshener is a product people can buy which is meant to make rooms smell pleasant.

★ **spray** [sprei] v. 뿌리다; (작은 것을 아주 많이) 뿌리다; n. 물보라; 분무기; 뿌리기
If you spray a liquid somewhere or if it sprays somewhere, drops of the liquid cover a place or shower someone.

by oneself idiom 도움을 받지 않고; 혼자
If you do something by yourselves or all by yourselves, you do it without any help from anyone else.

★ **pine** [pain] n. 소나무
A pine tree or a pine is a tall tree which has very thin, sharp leaves and a fresh smell. Pine trees have leaves all year round.

★★ **hug** [hʌg] v. 껴안다, 포옹하다; n. 포옹
When you hug someone, you put your arms around them and hold them tightly, for example because you like them or are pleased to see them.

★ **dessert** [dizə́:rt] n. 디저트, 후식
Dessert is something sweet, such as fruit or a pudding, that you eat at the end of a meal.

Chapter 2

1. What did Junie B. like about the nursery?

A. It had animal wallpaper.

B. It had a colorful dresser.

C. It had a comfortable rocking chair.

D. It had a strong crib.

2. What did Junie B. think was unfair?

A. Her room was smaller than the nursery.

B. She had to give the baby her old toys.

C. Only the baby got cool new things.

D. She was not allowed to help set up the baby's things.

3. Why didn't Junie B.'s parents pick a name for the baby yet?

A. They were too busy to decide on a name.

B. They did not think that picking a name was important.

C. They wanted a name that was interesting.

D. They could not agree on the same name.

4. What did Junie B.'s mom think of the name "Mrs. Gutzman"?

A. She thought that it would be hard to remember.

B. She thought that it would be funny.

C. She did not think that it was different enough.

D. She did not think that it was right.

5. What was Junie B. determined to do?

A. Become the baby's favorite person

B. Be the boss of the baby

C. Put on the baby's clothes

D. Take the baby's room

Check Your Reading Speed

1분에 몇 단어를 읽는지 리딩 속도를 측정해 보세요.

$$\frac{812 \text{ words}}{\text{reading time (} \quad \text{) sec}} \times 60 = (\quad) \text{ WPM}$$

Build Your Vocabulary

복습 **dumb** [dʌm] a. 멍청한, 바보 같은; 말을 못하는
If you say that something is dumb, you think that it is silly and annoying.

★★★ **fix** [fiks] v. 준비하다, 마련하다; 고치다; 정하다
If you fix something for someone, you arrange for it to happen or you organize it for them.

★ **nursery** [nə́:rsəri] n. 아기방; 탁아소, 유치원
A nursery is a room in a family home in which the young children of the family sleep or play.

복습 **except** [iksépt] conj. ~이지만, ~라는 점만 제외하면; prep. ~ 외에는; v. 제외하다
You can use except to introduce a statement that makes what you have just said seem less true or less possible.

복습 **stuff** [stʌf] n. 것, 물건, 일; v. 채워 넣다; 쑤셔 넣다
You can use stuff to refer to things such as a substance, a collection of things, events, or ideas, or the contents of something in a general way without mentioning the thing itself by name.

dresser [drésər] n. 서랍장; 화장대
A dresser is a piece of bedroom furniture with a lot of drawers.

★ **knob** [nab] n. (동그란) 손잡이; 혹, 마디
A knob is a round handle on a door or drawer which you use in order to open or close it.

⁑ **shade** [ʃeid] n. (전등의) 갓; 그늘; 블라인드; 색조; 음영; v. 그늘지게 하다
A shade is a covering that is put over an electric light in order to make it less bright.

⋆ **rock** [rak] v. 흔들리다, 흔들다; n. 바위; 돌멩이 (rocking chair n. 흔들의자)
A rocking chair is a chair that is built on two curved pieces of wood so that you can rock yourself backward and forward when you are sitting in it.

crib [krib] n. 아기 침대; 구유, 여물통
A crib is a bed for a small baby.

⁑ **bar** [baːr] n. 막대; 장애물; v. 빗장을 지르다; 막다, 차단하다
A bar is a long, straight, stiff piece of metal. Bars are often used to stop someone from getting through a space.

⋆ **cage** [keidʒ] n. 우리; 새장; v. 우리에 가두다
A cage is a structure of wire or metal bars in which birds or animals are kept.

wallpaper [wɔ́ːlpèipər] n. 벽지; v. 벽지를 바르다
Wallpaper is thick colored or patterned paper that is used for covering and decorating the walls of rooms.

⋆ **jungle** [dʒʌŋgl] n. 밀림 (지대), 정글
A jungle is a forest in a tropical country where large numbers of tall trees and plants grow very close together.

⋆ **paste** [peist] v. 풀칠하다, 풀로 붙이다; n. 반죽, 풀; 연고
If you paste something on a surface, you put glue or paste on it and stick it on the surface.

⁑ **fair** [fɛər] a. 공정한; 타당한; 아름다운; ad. 공정하게, 타당하게; n. 축제; 박람회
Something or someone that is fair is reasonable, right, and just.

⋆ **junk** [dʒʌŋk] n. 쓸모없는 물건, 폐물, 쓰레기; v. 폐물로 처분하다
Junk is things that you do not want or like.

★ **tease** [ti:z] v. 놀리다, 장난하다; (동물을) 못 살게 굴다; n. 장난, 놀림
To tease someone means to laugh at them or make jokes about them in order to embarrass, annoy, or upset them.

★★ **bend** [bend] v. (bent-bent) (몸·머리를) 굽히다, 숙이다; 구부리다; n. (도로·강의) 굽이, 굽은 곳
When you bend, you move the top part of your body downward and forward.

복습 **hug** [hʌg] v. 껴안다, 포옹하다; n. 포옹
When you hug someone, you put your arms around them and hold them tightly, for example because you like them or are pleased to see them.

★★ **stomach** [stʌ́mək] n. 배, 복부, 위(胃)
You can refer to the front part of your body below your waist as your stomach.

★ **lap** [læp] n. 무릎; v. 휘감다, 두르다; 겹치게 하다
If you have something on your lap when you are sitting down, it is on top of your legs that forms a flat surface.

★★★ **fit** [fit] v. (모양·크기가) 맞다; 적절하다; 어울리게 하다; a. 적합한, 알맞은; 건강한
If someone or something fits somewhere, they are small enough or the right size and shape to go there.

★ **clap** [klæp] v. 박수를 치다; (갑자기·재빨리) 놓다; n. 박수; 쿵 하는 소리
When you clap, you hit your hands together to show appreciation or attract attention.

★ **cafeteria** [kæfətíəriə] n. 구내식당
A cafeteria is a restaurant in public buildings where you choose your food from a counter and take it to your table after paying for it.

★ **frown** [fraun] v. 얼굴을 찡그리다; 눈살을 찌푸리다; n. 찡그림, 찌푸림
When someone frowns, their eyebrows become drawn together, because they are annoyed or puzzled.

복습 **holler** [hálər] v. 소리 지르다, 고함치다; n. 고함, 외침
If you holler, you shout loudly.

stick [stik] v. (sticked/stuck-sticked/stuck) 꽂히다, 찌르다; 움직이지 않다; 붙이다; n. 막대기
If something sticks in your mind, you remember it for a long time.

tiny [táini] a. 아주 작은
Something or someone that is tiny is extremely small.

scrunch [skrʌntʃ] v. 찡그리다; 웅크리다; 더 작게 만들다
If you scrunch your face or part of your face, you make it into a tight shape in order to show an emotion.

teeny [tíːni] a. 아주 작은
If you describe something as teeny, you are emphasizing that it is very small.

get used to idiom ~에 익숙해지다
If you get used to something or someone, you become familiar with them or get to know them, so that you no longer feel that they are unusual or surprising.

pajamas [pədʒáːməz] n. (바지와 상의로 된) 잠옷
A pair of pajamas consists of loose trousers and a loose jacket that people wear in bed.

weensy [wíːnsi] a. 조그마한
Something or someone that is weensy is very small.

piggie [pígi] n. (= piggy) 발가락; 새끼 돼지
Piggies are a child's word for toes.

toe [tou] n. 발가락
Your toes are the five movable parts at the end of each foot.

boss [bɔːs] n. 두목, 보스; (직장의) 상사; v. ~를 쥐고 흔들다
If you are the boss in a group or relationship, you are the person with a powerful position in the group or relationship.

★ **snap** [snæp] v. 탁 소리 내다; (화난 목소리로) 딱딱거리다; 툭 하고 부러지다; n. 탁 하는 소리
If you snap your fingers, you make a sharp sound by moving your middle finger quickly across your thumb, for example, in order to accompany music or to order someone to do something.

★★★ **hall** [hɔ:l] n. (건물 내의) 복도, 통로; (크고 넓은) 방, 홀, 회관
A hall in a building is a long passage with doors into rooms on both sides of it.

★ **whisper** [hwíspər] v. 속삭이다, 소곤거리다; n. 속삭임, 소곤거리는 소리
When you whisper, you say something very quietly, using your breath rather than your throat, so that only one person can hear you.

Chapter 3

1. Why did Junie B. stay at her grandparents' house?

A. It was a special holiday.

B. She stayed there every week.

C. Her grandpa needed help.

D. Her parents went to the hospital.

2. What did Junie B. and her grandpa do together?

A. They took out all of her grandma's clothes.

B. They ate dessert for dinner.

C. They watched a scary movie.

D. They told each other secrets.

3. Why didn't Junie B. sleep well at night?

A. She thought that there was something under the bed.

B. She was worried about her mother.

C. She was wondering what the baby would look like.

D. She could hear her grandpa snoring.

4. What did NOT happen in the morning?

A. Junie B.'s grandpa made waffles for breakfast.

B. Junie B. had time to play with her grandpa.

C. Junie B.'s mom and dad called from the hospital.

D. Junie B.'s grandma returned home.

5. What did Junie B.'s grandma say that surprised her?

A. Her brother was a cute monkey.

B. Her brother had no hair.

C. Her brother already cried a lot.

D. Her brother was the smallest baby in the hospital.

Check Your Reading Speed

1분에 몇 단어를 읽는지 리딩 속도를 측정해 보세요.

$$\frac{\text{762 words}}{\text{reading time (}\qquad\text{) sec}} \times 60 = (\qquad) \text{ WPM}$$

Build Your Vocabulary

복습 **that's all** idiom 그게 다이다, 그뿐이다
You can say 'that's all' at the end of a sentence when you say that there is nothing more involved than what you have mentioned.

복습 **by oneself** idiom 혼자; 도움을 받지 않고
If you are by yourselves or all by yourselves, you are alone.

babysit [béibisit] v. (부모가 외출한 동안) 아이를 봐 주다
If you babysit for someone or babysit their children, you look after their children while they are out.

★★ **smoke** [smouk] v. (담배를) 피우다; 연기를 내뿜다; 질주하다; n. 연기
When someone smokes a cigarette, cigar, or pipe, they suck the smoke from it into their mouth and blow it out again.

real live [rí:əl làiv] a. 실물의, 진짜의
You use real live to say that someone or something is present or exists, when you want to indicate that you think this is exciting and unusual or unexpected.

★ **yell** [jel] v. 고함치다, 소리 지르다; n. 고함, 외침
If you yell, you shout loudly, usually because you are excited, angry, or in pain.

★★★ **ride** [raid] n. 타기; (말·차량 등을) 타고 달리기; 놀이기구; v. (말·차량 등을) 타다
A ride is a trip on a horse or bicycle, or in a vehicle.

★ **feather** [féðər] n. (새의) 털, 깃털; v. 깃털로 덮다
A bird's feathers are the soft covering on its body. Each feather consists of a lot of smooth hairs on each side of a thin stiff center.

★ **heel** [hi:l] n. (pl.) 힐, 하이힐; 발뒤꿈치; (신발의) 굽
Heels are women's shoes that are raised very high at the back.

take off idiom (옷 등을) 벗다, 벗기다; (붙어 있던 것을) 떼어 내다; 이륙하다
If you take something off, you remove it, especially a piece of clothing from your body.

★ **crack** [kræk] v. 깨뜨리다, 부수다; 갈라지게 하다, 금이 가게 하다; n. (좁은) 틈; (갈라져 생긴) 금
If you crack something, you break it open or into pieces.

★ **refrigerator** [rifrídʒərèitər] n. 냉장고
A refrigerator is a large container which is kept cool inside, usually by electricity, so that the food and drink in it stays fresh.

p.j.'s [pí:dʒèiz] n. (= pajamas) (바지와 상의로 된) 잠옷
P.j.'s are the same as pajamas which consist of loose trousers and a loose jacket that people wear in bed.

★ **brush** [brʌʃ] v. 솔질을 하다; (솔이나 손으로) 털다; (붓을 이용하여) 바르다; n. 붓; 솔
If you brush something, you clean it or make it neat using a brush.

front tooth [frʌnt tú:θ] n. (pl. front teeth) 앞니
A front tooth is a tooth situated at the front of the mouth.

★ **tuck** [tʌk] v. (따뜻하게) 덮어 주다; 집어넣다, 끼워 넣다; 밀어 넣다; n. 주름, 단
If you tuck someone in, especially a child, you put them into bed and make sure that they are warm and comfortable by covering them well.

★ **scare** [skεər] v. 겁주다; 무서워하다; n. 불안(감); 놀람, 공포 (scared a. 겁먹은)
If you are scared of someone or something, you are frightened of them.

★ **closet** [klázit] n. 벽장
A closet is a piece of furniture with doors at the front and shelves inside, which is used for storing things.

복습 **hall** [hɔ:l] n. (건물 내의) 복도, 통로; (크고 넓은) 방, 홀, 회관
A hall in a building is a long passage with doors into rooms on both sides of it.

★★ **imagination** [imædʒənéiʃən] n. 상상, 상상력; 착각; 창의력
Your imagination is the part of your mind which allows you to form pictures or ideas of things that do not necessarily exist in real life.

run wild idiom 제멋대로 전개되다, 제멋대로 자라다; (아이·동물이) 제멋대로 날뛰다
If something runs wild, it is not controlled and operates in an extremely free way.

drooly [drú:li] a. 침을 흘리는
If you describe a person or animal as drooly, saliva drops slowly from their mouth.

★ **claw** [klɔ:] n. (동물·새의) 발톱; v. 헤치며 나아가다; (손톱·발톱으로) 할퀴다
The claws of a bird or animal are the thin, hard, curved nails at the end of its feet.

sag [sæg] v. 축 처지다, 축 늘어지다; 약화되다, 줄어들다; n. 늘어짐, 처짐
When something sags, it hangs down loosely or sinks downward in the middle.

★ **sniff** [snif] v. 냄새를 맡다; 코를 훌쩍이다; n. 냄새 맡기; 콧방귀 뀌기
If you sniff something or sniff at it, you smell it by taking air in through your nose.

★★ **pour** [pɔ:r] v. 붓다, 따르다; 마구 쏟아지다; 쏟아져 나오다
If you pour a liquid or other substance, you make it flow steadily out of a container by holding the container at an angle.

복습 **kindergarten** [kíndərgà:rtn] n. 유치원
A kindergarten is a school or class for children aged 4 to 6 years old. It prepares them to go into the first grade.

★ **giant** [dʒáiənt] a. 거대한, 엄청나게 큰; 비범한; n. 거인
Something that is described as giant is extremely large, strong, powerful, or important.

★ **swing** [swiŋ] v. (swung-swung) 흔들다, 흔들리다; 휘두르다; n. 흔들기; 그네
If something swings or if you swing it, it moves repeatedly backward and forward or from side to side from a fixed point.

복습 **toe** [tou] n. 발가락
Your toes are the five movable parts at the end of each foot.

★ **tug** [tʌg] v. (세게) 잡아당기다; n. (갑자기 세게) 잡아당김
If you tug something or tug at it, you give it a quick and usually strong pull.

oodles [ú:dlz] n. (pl.) 많음, 풍부함
If you say that there are oodles of something, you are emphasizing that there is a very large quantity of it.

be supposed to idiom ~하기로 되어 있다
If you are supposed to do something, you are expected or required to do it according to a rule, a custom or an arrangement.

baldy [bɔ́:ldi] n. 대머리인 사람
People sometimes refer to someone who has lost or is losing the hair on their head as a baldy, in a friendly or humorous way.

★ **grab** [græb] v. (와락·단단히) 붙잡다; 급히 ~하다; n. 와락 잡아채려고 함
If you grab something, you take or hold someone or something with your hand suddenly, firmly, or roughly.

★ **stamp** [stæmp] v. (발을) 구르다; 쾅쾅거리며 걷다; (도장 등을) 찍다; n. 쿵쾅거리기; 도장
If you stamp or stamp your foot, you lift your foot and put it down very hard on the ground, for example because you are angry.

복습 **frown** [fraun] v. 얼굴을 찡그리다; 눈살을 찌푸리다; n. 찡그림, 찌푸림
When someone frowns, their eyebrows become drawn together, because they are annoyed or puzzled.

복습 **bend** [bend] v. (bent-bent) (몸·머리를) 굽히다, 숙이다; 구부리다; n. (도로·강의) 굽이, 굽은 곳
When you bend, you move the top part of your body downward and forward.

★★★ **honest** [ánist] ad. 정말로, 틀림없이; a. 솔직한; 정직한
You say 'honest' before or after a statement to emphasize that you are telling the truth and that you want people to believe you.

★ **truly** [trú:li] ad. 정말로, 진심으로
You use truly to emphasize that feelings are genuine and sincere.

복습 **whisper** [hwíspər] v. 속삭이다, 소곤거리다; n. 속삭임, 소곤거리는 소리
When you whisper, you say something very quietly, using your breath rather than your throat, so that only one person can hear you.

twirl [twə:rl] v. 빙글빙글 돌다, 빙글빙글 돌리다; n. 회전
If you twirl, you turn around and around quickly, for example when you are dancing.

Chapter 4

1. Why was Grace angry?

A. She did not like her new shoes.

B. She had a bad time on the bus.

C. Junie B. forgot to call her yesterday.

D. Junie B. got her in trouble at school.

2. What did Junie B. say to Grace?

A. She wanted to make Grace feel better.

B. She would ride the bus with Grace next time.

C. She would make up a lie about Grace.

D. She would not tell Grace her secret.

3. Why did Lucille keep talking to Junie B.?

A. She wanted Junie B. and Grace to be friends again.

B. She wanted to know Junie B.'s secret.

C. She needed help printing her numbers.

D. She needed an idea for Show and Tell.

4. Why couldn't Junie B. go first for Show and Tell?

A. She was not being polite.

B. She did not finish her work.

C. Mrs. did not see her raise her hand.

D. William was already first on the list.

5. What was true about William?

A. He thought that the crickets were alive.

B. He did not think that the crickets were real.

C. He taught the crickets some tricks.

D. He was scared of crickets.

Check Your Reading Speed

1분에 몇 단어를 읽는지 리딩 속도를 측정해 보세요.

$$\frac{\text{747 words}}{\text{reading time (} \quad \text{) sec}} \times 60 = (\qquad) \text{ WPM}$$

Build Your Vocabulary

복습 **kindergarten** [kíndərgà:rtn] n. 유치원
A kindergarten is a school or class for children aged 4 to 6 years old. It prepares them to go into the first grade.

★★★ **exact** [igzǽkt] a. 정확한; 꼼꼼한, 빈틈없는 (exactly ad. 정확히, 틀림없이)
You use exactly before an amount, number, or position to emphasize that it is no more, no less, or no different from what you are stating.

★ **fingernail** [fíŋgərnèil] n. 손톱
Your fingernails are the thin hard areas at the end of each of your fingers.

glossy [glási] a. 광택이 나는, 번질번질한
Glossy means smooth and shiny.

복습 **except** [iksépt] conj. ~이지만, ~라는 점만 제외하면; prep. ~ 외에는; v. 제외하다
You can use except to introduce a statement that makes what you have just said seem less true or less possible.

★★ **wave** [weiv] v. (손·팔을) 흔들다; 손짓하다; 흔들리다; n. (팔·손·몸을) 흔들기; 파도, 물결
If you wave or wave your hand, you move your hand from side to side in the air, usually in order to say hello or goodbye to someone.

복습 **that's all** idiom 그게 다이다, 그뿐이다
You can say 'that's all' at the end of a sentence when you say that there is nothing more involved than what you have mentioned.

brand-new [brænd-njúː] a. 아주 새로운, 신상품의
A brand-new object is completely new.

복습 **dumb** [dʌm] a. 멍청한, 바보 같은; 말을 못하는
If you call a person dumb, you mean that they are stupid or foolish.

복습 **ride** [raid] v. (rode-ridden) (말·차량 등을) 타다; n. (말·차량 등을) 타고 달리기; 타기; 놀이기구
When you ride a vehicle such as a car, you travel in it, especially as a passenger.

icky [íki] a. (끈적끈적하게) 기분 나쁜, 불쾌한
If you describe something as icky, you mean that it is unpleasant, especially wet and sticky.

bob [bab] v. (고개를) 까닥거리다; 위아래로 움직이다; n. (머리·몸을) 까닥거림
When you bob your head, you move it quickly up and down once, for example when you greet someone.

★★ **polite** [pəláit] a. 예의 바른, 공손한, 정중한; 예의상의
Someone who is polite has good manners and behaves in a way that is socially correct and not rude to other people.

★ **involve** [inválv] v. 관련시키다, 연루시키다; 수반하다, 포함하다
If a situation or activity involves someone, they are taking part in it.

★★ **print** [print] v. (글자를) 인쇄체로 쓰다; 인쇄하다; n. (인쇄된) 활자
If you print words, you write in letters that are not joined together and that look like the letters in a book or newspaper.

★ **neighbor** [néibər] n. 옆자리 사람; 이웃 (사람); v. 이웃하다, 인접하다
You can refer to the person who is standing or sitting next to you as your neighbor.

복습 **snap** [snæp] v. 탁 소리 내다; (화난 목소리로) 딱딱거리다; 툭 하고 부러지다; n. 탁 하는 소리
If you snap your fingers, you make a sharp sound by moving your middle finger quickly across your thumb, for example, in order to accompany music or to order someone to do something.

복습 **holler** [hálər] v. 소리 지르다, 고함치다; n. 고함, 외침
If you holler, you shout loudly.

shush [ʃʌʃ] int. 쉿 (조용히 해); v. 조용히 하라고 말하다
You say 'shush' when you are telling someone to be quiet.

★ **pump** [pʌmp] v. 빠르게 움직이다, 흔들다; (펌프로) 퍼내다; n. 펌프, 심장
If something pumps, it moves quickly up and down or in and out.

복습 **be supposed to** idiom ~하기로 되어 있다
If you are supposed to do something, you are expected or required to do it according to a rule, a custom or an arrangement.

cry-baby [krái-bèibi] n. 울보
If you call a child a cry-baby, you mean that the child cries a lot for no good reason.

★★ **beat** [bi:t] v. 때리다; 이기다; (심장이) 고동치다; n. 리듬; 고동, 맥박
If someone beats a person up, they hit or kick the person many times.

★★ **jar** [dʒa:r] n. (잼·꿀 등을 담아 두는) 병; 단지; 항아리
A jar is a glass container with a lid that is used for storing food.

★ **cricket** [kríkit] n. [곤충] 귀뚜라미
A cricket is a small jumping insect that produces short, loud sounds by rubbing its wings together.

★ **tap** [tæp] v. (가볍게) 톡톡 두드리다; n. (가볍게) 두드리기
If you tap something, you hit it gently, and often repeatedly, especially making short, sharp noises.

fall apart idiom 다 부서지다, 허물어지다
If something falls apart, its parts separate from each other.

Chapter 5

1. What did Junie B. tell the class?

A. She had always wanted a little brother.

B. She saw a photo of her little brother.

C. Her brother was an actual monkey.

D. Her brother's name was Monkey.

2. How did Jim react to Junie B.'s news?

A. He was confused about it.

B. He was amazed by it.

C. He agreed with it.

D. He did not believe it.

3. How did Mrs. react to Junie B.'s words?

A. She laughed at Junie B.'s imagination.

B. She showed no interest in Junie B.'s news.

C. She was suspicious of Junie B's words.

D. She was sure that Junie B. was telling the truth.

4. How did Junie B. describe her brother's room?

A. It had a bed with bars.

B. It had many stuffed animals.

C. It had scary wallpaper.

D. It had a painting of a jungle.

5. What did Ricardo do?

A. He asked Junie B. to be his girlfriend.

B. He told Junie B. that monkeys were cool.

C. He asked Junie B. to bring her brother to school.

D. He told Junie B. that he had a pet monkey.

Check Your Reading Speed

1분에 몇 단어를 읽는지 리딩 속도를 측정해 보세요.

$$\frac{\text{416 words}}{\text{reading time (}\qquad\text{) sec}} \times 60 = (\qquad) \text{ WPM}$$

Build Your Vocabulary

★★ **business** [bíznis] n. (논의하거나 처리해야 할) 일; 사업, 장사; 사건
If you have business, you have important matters that you have to deal with or discuss.

★ **speedy** [spí:di] a. 빠른, 신속한
A speedy process, event, or action happens or is done very quickly.

복습 **clap** [klæp] v. 박수를 치다; (갑자기·재빨리) 놓다; n. 박수; 쿵 하는 소리
When you clap, you hit your hands together to show appreciation or attract attention.

squint [skwint] v. 눈을 가늘게 뜨고 보다; 곁눈질로 보다; n. 잠깐 봄; 사시
If you squint at something, you look at it with your eyes partly closed.

복습 **tiny** [táini] a. 아주 작은
Something or someone that is tiny is extremely small.

★★ **mean** [mi:n] a. 성질이 나쁜, 심술궂은; v. 의미하다
If you describe a person or animal as mean, you are saying that they are very bad-tempered and cruel.

★ **eyebrow** [áibràu] n. 눈썹
Your eyebrows are the lines of hair which grow above your eyes.

복습 **toe** [tou] n. 발가락
Your toes are the five movable parts at the end of each foot.

★ **fur** [fəːr] n. (동물의) 털; 모피
Fur is the thick and usually soft hair that grows on the bodies of many mammals.

복습 **wallpaper** [wɔ́ːlpèipər] n. 벽지; v. 벽지를 바르다
Wallpaper is thick colored or patterned paper that is used for covering and decorating the walls of rooms.

복습 **jungle** [dʒʌŋgl] n. 밀림 (지대), 정글
A jungle is a forest in a tropical country where large numbers of tall trees and plants grow very close together.

복습 **bar** [baːr] n. 막대; 장애물; v. 빗장을 지르다; 막다, 차단하다
A bar is a long, straight, stiff piece of metal. Bars are often used to stop someone from getting through a space.

★★ **bite** [bait] v. 물다; 베어 물다; n. 물기; 한 입
If an animal or person bites you, they use their teeth to hurt or injure you.

freckle [frekl] n. 주근깨
Freckles are small light brown spots on someone's skin, especially on their face.

★★ **pet** [pet] n. 반려동물; v. (다정하게) 어루만지다
A pet is an animal that you keep in your home to give you company and pleasure.

★ **giggle** [gigl] v. 킥킥거리다, 피식 웃다; n. 킥킥거림, 피식 웃음
If someone giggles, they laugh in a childlike way, because they are amused, nervous, or embarrassed.

복습 **wave** [weiv] v. (손·팔을) 흔들다; 흔들리다; n. (팔·손·몸을) 흔들기; 파도, 물결
If you wave or wave your hand, you move your hand from side to side in the air, usually in order to say hello or goodbye to someone.

★ **skip** [skip] v. 깡충깡충 뛰다; (일을) 거르다; 생략하다; n. 깡충깡충 뛰기
If you skip along, you move almost as if you are dancing, with a series of little jumps from one foot to the other.

Chapter 6

1. Why did Lucille let Junie B. wear her locket?

A. She wanted Junie B. to give it to her brother.

B. She wanted to be the first person to see Junie B.'s brother.

C. She thought that it would look pretty on Junie B.

D. She thought that it would bring Junie B. good luck.

2. What was Junie B.'s idea?

A. She could choose Lucille or Grace randomly.

B. Lucille could share her locket with Grace, too.

C. Grace could give Junie B. something nice, too.

D. Lucille and Grace could meet Junie B.'s brother together.

3. What did Grace say about her ring?

A. It was from her cereal.

B. It was very expensive.

C. She had worn it for a long time.

D. She made it herself.

4. What happened between Lucille and Grace?

A. They started to joke with each other.

B. They felt sorry for each other.

C. They were impressed by each other.

D. They competed with each other.

5. Why did Grace hesitate to give Junie B. her pink high tops?

A. They were actually her sister's shoes.

B. They were still new.

C. They were her favorite color.

D. They were a gift from her nanna.

Check Your Reading Speed

1분에 몇 단어를 읽는지 리딩 속도를 측정해 보세요.

$$\frac{\text{799 words}}{\text{reading time (\quad) sec}} \times 60 = (\quad) \text{ WPM}$$

Build Your Vocabulary

★ **recess** [risés] n. (학교의) 쉬는 시간; (의회·위원회 등의) 휴회 기간
A recess is a short period of time during the school day when children can play.

★ **subject** [sʌ́bdʒikt] n. 학과, 과목; 주제; a. ~될 수 있는
A subject is an area of knowledge or study, especially one that you study at school, college, or university.

★ **steam** [sti:m] n. 에너지, 화; 김, 증기; 추진력; v. 김을 내뿜다; 화내다, 발끈하다
If you let off steam, you get rid of your energy, anger, or strong emotions with physical activity or by behaving in a noisy or violent way.

복습 **holler** [hálər] v. 소리 지르다, 고함치다; n. 고함, 외침
If you holler, you shout loudly.

복습 **whisper** [hwíspər] v. 속삭이다, 소곤거리다; n. 속삭임, 소곤거리는 소리
When you whisper, you say something very quietly, using your breath rather than your throat, so that only one person can hear you.

복습 **dumb** [dʌm] a. 멍청한, 바보 같은; 말을 못하는
If you say that something is dumb, you think that it is silly and annoying.

★ **chain** [ʧein] n. 목걸이, 쇠줄; v. (사슬로) 묶다, 매다
A chain is a series of small metal rings connected to each other that is worn as a decoration.

beauteous [bjú:tiəs] a. 아름다운, 예쁜
If you describe something as beauteous, you mean that it is very attractive or pleasing.

nanna [nǽnə] n. 할머니; 유모
Some people refer to their grandmother as their nan or nanna.

bitty [bíti] a. 조그마한
If you describe someone or something as a little bitty person or thing, you are emphasizing that they are very small.

복습 **teeny** [tí:ni] a. 아주 작은
If you describe something as teeny, you are emphasizing that it is very small.

복습 **squint** [skwint] v. 눈을 가늘게 뜨고 보다; 곁눈질로 보다; n. 잠깐 봄; 사시
If you squint at something, you look at it with your eyes partly closed.

stomp [stamp] v. 쿵쿵거리며 걷다; 발을 구르며 춤추다
If you stomp somewhere, you walk there with very heavy steps, often because you are angry.

복습 **ride** [raid] v. (말·차량 등을) 타다; n. (말·차량 등을) 타고 달리기; 타기; 놀이기구
When you ride a vehicle such as a car, you travel in it, especially as a passenger.

복습 **shoulder** [ʃóuldər] n. 어깨; (옷의) 어깨 부분
Your shoulder is one of the two parts of your body between your neck and the top of your arms.

복습 **make a face** idiom 얼굴을 일그러뜨리다
If you make a face, you show a feeling such as dislike or disgust by putting an exaggerated expression on your face.

복습 **except** [iksépt] conj. ~이지만, ~라는 점만 제외하면; prep. ~ 외에는; v. 제외하다
You can use except to introduce a statement that makes what you have just said seem less true or less possible.

복습 **fair** [fɛər] a. 공정한; 타당한; 아름다운; ad. 공정하게, 타당하게; n. 축제; 박람회
Something or someone that is fair is reasonable, right, and just.

복습 **take off** idiom (옷 등을) 벗다, 벗기다; (붙어 있던 것을) 떼어 내다; 이륙하다
If you take something off, you remove it, especially a piece of clothing from your body.

sparkly [spáːrkli] a. 반짝반짝 빛나는; 불꽃을 튀기는; 활기 있는
Sparkly things are shining with small points of reflected light.

★ **shiny** [ʃáini] a. 빛나는, 반짝거리는
Shiny things are bright and reflect light.

★ **genuine** [dʒénjuin] a. 진짜의, 진품의; 진실한, 진심 어린
If something is genuine, it is real and exactly what it appears to be.

★ **fake** [feik] a. 모조의; 가짜의, 거짓된; n. 가짜, 모조품; v. ~인 척하다
Fake things are not real, but made to look or seem real.

★ **sleeve** [sliːv] n. (옷의) 소매, 소맷자락
The sleeves of a coat, shirt, or other item of clothing are the parts that cover your arms.

★★ **tie** [tai] n. 동점, 무승부; 넥타이; 끈; 유대; v. 묶다; 결부시키다; 동점을 이루다
A tie in a competition or game means a situation in which two or more people finish at the same time or score the same number of points.

★★ **waist** [weist] n. 허리
Your waist is the middle part of your body where it narrows slightly above your hips.

snack [snæk] n. 간식; v. 간식을 먹다
A snack is something such as a chocolate bar that you eat between meals.

high five [hài fáiv] n. 하이 파이브
If you give someone a high five, you put your hand up and hit their open hand with yours, especially after a victory or as a greeting.

★ **stare** [stɛər] v. 빤히 쳐다보다, 응시하다; n. 빤히 쳐다보기, 응시
If you stare at someone or something, you look at them for a long time.

★ **pat** [pæt] v. 쓰다듬다, 토닥거리다; n. 쓰다듬기, 토닥거리기
If you pat something or someone, you tap them lightly, usually with your hand held flat.

복습 **polite** [pəláit] a. 예의 바른, 공손한, 정중한; 예의상의 (politely ad. 예의 바르게)
Someone who is polite has good manners and behaves in a way that is socially correct and not rude to other people.

★★★ **turn** [tə:rn] n. 차례, 순번; 돌기; 전환; v. 돌다, 돌리다; 변하다
If it is your turn to do something, you now have the duty, chance, or right to do it, when other people have done it before you or will do it after you.

Chapter 7

1. According to Junie B., why did Lucille have to give up her chair?

A. Junie B. sat in it first.

B. They had to take turns with it.

C. Junie B. liked red more.

D. That was the rule.

2. Why was Junie B. excited to see Mrs. Gutzman?

A. She could get three snacks today.

B. She wanted to show off her new things.

C. Mrs. Gutzman made the best cookies.

D. Mrs. Gutzman was always nice to her.

3. What did Lucille say to Mrs.?

A. She was not hungry for a snack.

B. She lost her snack ticket outside.

C. She had to give Junie B. her snack ticket.

D. She wanted Junie B. to have her snack ticket.

4. What did Mrs. notice about Grace?

A. She was being quieter than usual.

B. She was crying for no reason.

C. She was wearing a different pair of shoes.

D. She was walking in her socks.

5. What did Mrs. make Junie B. do?

A. Throw away the locket and ring

B. Go to the principal's office

C. Write a note to her friends

D. Explain to her mom what happened

Check Your Reading Speed

1분에 몇 단어를 읽는지 리딩 속도를 측정해 보세요.

$$\frac{688 \text{ words}}{\text{reading time (} \quad \text{) sec}} \times 60 = (\quad) \text{ WPM}$$

Build Your Vocabulary

복습 **brand-new** [brænd-njú:] a. 아주 새로운, 신상품의
A brand-new object is completely new.

★ **slide** [slaid] v. 미끄러지다; 미끄러지듯이 움직이다; n. 미끄러짐; 떨어짐
When something slides somewhere or when you slide it there, it moves there smoothly over or against something.

복습 **tap** [tæp] v. (가볍게) 톡톡 두드리다; n. (가볍게) 두드리기
If you tap something, you hit it gently, and often repeatedly, especially making short, sharp noises.

★★ **upset** [ʌpsét] a. 속상한, 마음이 상한; v. 속상하게 하다
If you are upset, you are unhappy or disappointed because something unpleasant has happened to you.

복습 **pat** [pæt] v. 쓰다듬다, 토닥거리다; n. 쓰다듬기, 토닥거리기
If you pat something or someone, you tap them lightly, usually with your hand held flat.

★★★ **rule** [ru:l] n. 규칙, 규정; 지배, 통치; v. 지배하다, 통치하다
Rules are instructions that tell you what you are allowed to do and what you are not allowed to do.

복습 **shoulder** [ʃóuldər] n. 어깨; (옷의) 어깨 부분
Your shoulder is one of the two parts of your body between your neck and the top of your arms.

★ **cash** [kæʃ] n. 현금, 돈
Cash is money in the form of notes and coins.

★ **purse** [pəːrs] n. (작은) 지갑; 손가방; v. (입술을) 오므리다
A purse is a very small bag that people, especially women, keep their money in.

bulletin board [búlitən bɔːrd] n. 게시판
A bulletin board is a board which is usually attached to a wall in order to display notices giving information about something.

★ **sprinkle** [spriŋkl] v. 뿌리다; 간간이 섞다; 비가 보슬보슬 오다; n. 뿌려진 것; 보슬비
If you sprinkle a thing with something such as a liquid or powder, you scatter the liquid or powder over it.

복습 **shiny** [ʃáini] a. 빛나는, 반짝거리는
Shiny things are bright and reflect light.

★ **glitter** [glítər] n. (장식용) 반짝이; 반짝반짝 하는 빛; v. 반짝반짝 빛나다; (눈이) 번득이다
Glitter consists of tiny, shining pieces of metal. It is glued to things for decoration.

복습 **paste** [peist] v. 풀로 붙이다, 풀칠하다; n. 반죽, 풀; 연고
If you paste something on a surface, you put glue or paste on it and stick it on the surface.

복습 **eyebrow** [áibràu] n. 눈썹
Your eyebrows are the lines of hair which grow above your eyes.

confiscate [kánfəskèit] v. 압수하다, 몰수하다
If you confiscate something from someone, you take it away from them, usually as a punishment.

복습 **jar** [dʒaːr] n. (잼·꿀 등을 담아 두는) 병; 단지; 항아리
A jar is a glass container with a lid that is used for storing food.

yank [jæŋk] v. 홱 잡아당기다; n. 홱 잡아당기기
If you yank someone or something somewhere, you pull them there suddenly and with a lot of force.

★★ **knock** [nak] v. (문 등을) 두드리다; 치다, 부딪치다; n. 문 두드리는 소리; 부딪침
If you knock on something such as a door or window, you hit it, usually several times, to attract someone's attention.

★ **hurray** [həréi] int. 만세!
People sometimes shout 'hurray' when they are very happy and excited about something.

복습 **snack** [snæk] n. 간식; v. 간식을 먹다
A snack is something such as a chocolate bar that you eat between meals.

복습 **stare** [stɛər] v. 빤히 쳐다보다, 응시하다; n. 빤히 쳐다보기, 응시
If you stare at someone or something, you look at them for a long time.

★★ **extra** [ékstrə] a. 여분의; 추가의; 특별한; n. 추가되는 것; ad. 특별히
You use extra to describe an amount, person, or thing that is added to others of the same kind, or that can be added to others of the same kind.

★ **playground** [pléigràund] n. (학교의) 운동장; 놀이터
A playground is a piece of land, at school or in a public area, where children can play.

복습 **fold** [fould] v. (두 손·팔 등을) 끼다; 접다, 접히다; n. 주름; 접힌 부분
(fold one's arms idiom 팔짱을 끼다)
If you fold your arms or hands, you bring them together and cross or link them, for example, over your chest.

squinty [skwínti] a. 눈을 가늘게 뜨고 보는; 흘겨보는; 사시의
If you describe someone's eyes as squinty, you mean that their eyes are directed to one side with or as if with doubt, suspicion or envy.

★ **peep** [pi:p] v. 살짝 보다, 훔쳐보다; 살짝 보이다; n. 훔쳐보기, 살짝 봄
If you peep or peep at something, you take a quick look at it, often secretly and quietly.

복습 **scare** [skɛər] v. 겁주다; 무서워하다; n. 불안(감); 놀람, 공포 (scared a. 겁먹은)
If you are scared of someone or something, you are frightened of them.

복습 **bend** [bend] v. (bent-bent) (몸·머리를) 굽히다, 숙이다; 구부리다; n. (도로·강의) 굽이, 굽은 곳
When you bend, you move the top part of your body downward and forward.

roll one's eyes idiom 눈을 굴리다
If you roll your eyes or if your eyes roll, they move round and upward to show you are bored or annoyed.

복습 **hall** [hɔːl] n. (건물 내의) 복도, 통로; (크고 넓은) 방, 홀, 회관
A hall in a building is a long passage with doors into rooms on both sides of it.

복습 **genuine** [dʒénjuin] a. 진짜의, 진품의; 진실한, 진심 어린
If something is genuine, it is real and exactly what it appears to be.

복습 **fake** [feik] a. 모조의; 가짜의, 거짓된; n. 가짜, 모조품; v. ~인 척하다
Fake things are not real, but made to look or seem real.

복습 **boss** [bɔːs] n. 두목, 보스; (직장의) 상사; v. ~를 쥐고 흔들다
If you are the boss in a group or relationship, you are the person with a powerful position in the group or relationship.

★ **principal** [prínsəpəl] n. 교장; a. 주요한, 주된
The principal of a school or college is the person in charge of the school or college.

★★★ **march** [maːrtʃ] v. (급히) 걸어가다; (강요해서) 데려가다; 행진하다; n. 행진; 3월
If you say that someone marches somewhere, you mean that they walk there quickly and in a determined way.

Chapter 8

1. Why didn't Junie B. like the principal's office?

A. It had uncomfortable chairs.

B. It was dark and silent.

C. It was a place for bad kids.

D. It was far from her classroom.

2. What did she do when she met with the principal?

A. She made up an interesting story.

B. She talked about everything that had happened.

C. She asked when she could go home.

D. She said that she was sorry for causing trouble.

3. What did the principal realize about Grandma Miller?

A. She did not really think that the baby was cute.

B. She did not really mean that the baby was a monkey.

C. She knew that Junie B. would get confused.

D. She knew that Junie B. loved monkeys.

4. Why did the principal call Grandma Miller?

A. To convince Junie B. that he was right

B. To ask if he could see Junie B.'s brother

C. To request that Grandma Miller stop lying

D. To tell Grandma Miller to come to the school

5. How did Junie B. feel after the phone call?

A. She still could not wait to meet her brother.

B. She was thankful that her brother was not a monkey.

C. She was not sure who she should believe.

D. She felt sad to know the truth.

Check Your Reading Speed

1분에 몇 단어를 읽는지 리딩 속도를 측정해 보세요.

$$\frac{\text{881 words}}{\text{reading time (\qquad) sec}} \times 60 = (\qquad) \text{ WPM}$$

Build Your Vocabulary

복습 **principal** [prínsəpəl] n. 교장; a. 주요한, 주된
The principal of a school or college is the person in charge of the school or college.

scary [skέəri] a. 무서운, 겁나는
Something that is scary is rather frightening.

★★ **type** [taip] v. 타자를 치다, 입력하다; 분류하다; n. 유형, 종류
If you type something, you write it using a computer keyboard or typewriter.

★ **row** [rou] n. 열, 줄; 노 젓기; v. 노를 젓다
A row of things or people is a number of them arranged in a line.

plop [plap] v. 털썩 주저앉히다, 주저앉다; 떨어뜨리다; 퐁당 하고 떨어지다; n. 퐁당 (하는 소리)
If someone plops or you plop them, they sit down or land heavily or without taking care.

복습 **whisper** [hwíspər] v. 속삭이다, 소곤거리다; n. 속삭임, 소곤거리는 소리
When you whisper, you say something very quietly, using your breath rather than your throat, so that only one person can hear you.

peek [pi:k] v. (재빨리) 훔쳐보다; 살짝 보이다; n. 엿보기
If you peek at something or someone, you have a quick look at them, often secretly.

복습 **sleeve** [sli:v] n. (옷의) 소매, 소맷자락
The sleeves of a coat, shirt, or other item of clothing are the parts that cover your arms.

복습 **knock** [nak] v. (문 등을) 두드리다; 치다, 부딪치다; n. 문 두드리는 소리; 부딪침
If you knock on something such as a door or window, you hit it, usually several times, to attract someone's attention.

복습 **pump** [pʌmp] v. 빠르게 움직이다, 흔들다; (펌프로) 퍼내다; n. 펌프, 심장
If something pumps, it moves quickly up and down or in and out.

tattletale [tǽtltèil] n. 수다쟁이, 고자질쟁이; a. 고자질하는, 비밀을 폭로하는
A tattletale is a child who tells an adult what another child has done wrong.

복습 **baldy** [bɔ́:ldi] n. 대머리인 사람
People sometimes refer to someone who has lost or is losing the hair on their head as a baldy, in a friendly or humorous way.

★ **rubber** [rʌ́bər] n. 고무; a. 고무의
Rubber is a strong, waterproof, elastic substance made from the juice of a tropical tree or produced chemically.

복습 **by oneself** idiom 혼자; 도움을 받지 않고
If you are by yourselves or all by yourselves, you are alone.

복습 **take off** idiom (옷 등을) 벗다, 벗기다; (붙어 있던 것을) 떼어 내다; 이륙하다
If you take something off, you remove it, especially a piece of clothing from your body.

shoot one's mouth off idiom 지껄이다; 우쭐거리며 말하다
If you shoot your mouth off, you talk about something that you should not talk about or that you know nothing about.

복습 **fold** [fould] v. (두 손·팔 등을) 끼다; 접다, 접히다; n. 주름; 접힌 부분
(fold one's arms idiom 팔짱을 끼다)
If you fold your arms or hands, you bring them together and cross or link them, for example, over your chest.

복습 **except** [iksépt] conj. ~이지만, ~라는 점만 제외하면; prep. ~ 외에는; v. 제외하다
You can use except to introduce a statement that makes what you have just said seem less true or less possible.

복습 **honest** [ánist] ad. 정말로, 틀림없이; a. 솔직한; 정직한
You say 'honest' before or after a statement to emphasize that you are telling the truth and that you want people to believe you.

복습 **truly** [trú:li] ad. 정말로, 진심으로
You use truly to emphasize that feelings are genuine and sincere.

복습 **recess** [risés] n. (학교의) 쉬는 시간; (의회·위원회 등의) 휴회 기간
A recess is a short period of time during the school day when children can play.

복습 **stuff** [stʌf] n. 것, 물건, 일; v. 채워 넣다; 쑤셔 넣다
You can use stuff to refer to things such as a substance, a collection of things, events, or ideas, or the contents of something in a general way without mentioning the thing itself by name.

복습 **snack** [snæk] n. 간식; v. 간식을 먹다
A snack is something such as a chocolate bar that you eat between meals.

복습 **dumb** [dʌm] a. 멍청한, 바보 같은; 말을 못하는
If you call a person dumb, you mean that they are stupid or foolish.

복습 **march** [ma:rʧ] v. (강요해서) 데려가다; (급히) 걸어가다; 행진하다; n. 행진; 3월
If you march someone somewhere, you force them to walk there with you, for example by holding their arm tightly.

★ **smooth** [smu:ð] v. 매끈하게 하다, 반듯하게 펴다; a. 매끈한; 부드러운; (소리가) 감미로운
If you smooth something, you move your hands over its surface to make it smooth and flat.

★ **rub** [rʌb] v. (손·손수건 등을 대고) 문지르다; (두 손 등을) 맞비비다; n. 문지르기, 비비기
If you rub a part of your body, you move your hand or fingers backward and forward over it while pressing firmly.

복습 **exact** [igzǽkt] a. 정확한; 꼼꼼한, 빈틈없는 (exactly ad. 정확히, 틀림없이)
You use exactly when you want to emphasize that something is correct in every way or in every detail.

복습 **scrunch** [skrʌnʧ] v. 찡그리다; 웅크리다; 더 작게 만들다
If you scrunch your face or part of your face, you make it into a tight shape in order to show an emotion.

복습 **frown** [fraun] v. 얼굴을 찡그리다; 눈살을 찌푸리다; n. 찡그림, 찌푸림
When someone frowns, their eyebrows become drawn together, because they are annoyed or puzzled.

★ **hairy** [hέəri] a. 털이 많은, 털투성이의
Someone or something that is hairy is covered with hairs.

복습 **fur** [fəːr] n. (동물의) 털; 모피
Fur is the thick and usually soft hair that grows on the bodies of many mammals.

복습 **toe** [tou] n. 발가락
Your toes are the five movable parts at the end of each foot.

droopy [drúːpi] a. 지친, 의기소침한; 축 늘어진
If you feel droopy, you start to feel less happy and energetic.

복습 **cage** [keidʒ] n. 우리; 새장; v. 우리에 가두다
A cage is a structure of wire or metal bars in which birds or animals are kept.

복습 **wallpaper** [wɔ́ːlpèipər] n. 벽지; v. 벽지를 바르다
Wallpaper is thick colored or patterned paper that is used for covering and decorating the walls of rooms.

복습 **jungle** [dʒʌŋgl] n. 밀림 (지대), 정글
A jungle is a forest in a tropical country where large numbers of tall trees and plants grow very close together.

★★ **regular** [régjulər] a. 일반적인, 평범한; 규칙적인; n. 단골손님, 고정 고객
Regular is used to mean 'normal.'

hang up idiom 전화를 끊다; ~을 중지하다
To hang up means to end a telephone conversation, often very suddenly.

복습 **bend** [bend] v. (bent-bent) (몸·머리를) 굽히다, 숙이다; 구부리다; n. (도로·강의) 굽이, 굽은 곳
When you bend, you move the top part of your body downward and forward.

★ **tissue** [tíʃuː] n. 화장지; (세포) 조직
A tissue is a piece of thin soft paper that you use to blow your nose.

Chapter 9

1. What did the principal tell the class?

A. Silly expressions should not be used.

B. Some expressions can be unclear.

C. Anyone can have good luck.

D. All ducks bring good luck.

2. How did the kids react?

A. They had difficulty understanding the principal's point.

B. They described how different animals act.

C. They came up with new names for their family members.

D. They thought of fun examples that they had heard.

3. What happened by the end of the school day?

A. Mrs. took away the red chair.

B. Ricardo agreed to be Junie B.'s boyfriend.

C. Junie B. was friends with Lucille and Grace again.

D. Junie B. forgot about her new brother.

4. When did Junie B. finally meet her brother?

A. When she went out of the school

B. When she opened the car door

C. When she got off the bus

D. When she walked into her house

5. What did Junie B. think of her brother?

A. He was better than a monkey.

B. He was louder than a monkey.

C. He was cute like a monkey.

D. He was smelly like a monkey.

Check Your Reading Speed

1분에 몇 단어를 읽는지 리딩 속도를 측정해 보세요.

$$\frac{\text{754 words}}{\text{reading time (\qquad) sec}} \times 60 = (\qquad) \text{ WPM}$$

Build Your Vocabulary

복습 **stuff** [stʌf] n. 것, 물건, 일; v. 채워 넣다; 쑤셔 넣다

You can use stuff to refer to things such as a substance, a collection of things, events, or ideas, or the contents of something in a general way without mentioning the thing itself by name.

복습 **principal** [prínsəpəl] n. 교장; a. 주요한, 주된

The principal of a school or college is the person in charge of the school or college.

복습 **clap** [klæp] v. 박수를 치다; (갑자기·재빨리) 놓다; n. 박수; 쿵 하는 소리

When you clap, you hit your hands together to show appreciation or attract attention.

복습 **giant** [dʒáiənt] a. 거대한, 엄청나게 큰; 비범한; n. 거인

Something that is described as giant is extremely large, strong, powerful, or important.

★★ **attention** [əténʃən] n. 주의, 주목; 관심, 흥미; int. 알립니다, 주목하세요

If you give someone or something your attention, you look at it, listen to it, or think about it carefully.

★ **fist** [fist] n. 주먹

Your hand is referred to as your fist when you have bent your fingers in toward the palm in order to hit someone, to make an angry gesture, or to hold something.

복습 **dumb** [dʌm] a. 멍청한, 바보 같은; 말을 못하는
If you call a person dumb, you mean that they are stupid or foolish.

복습 **holler** [hálər] v. 소리 지르다, 고함치다; n. 고함, 외침
If you holler, you shout loudly.

복습 **frown** [fraun] v. 얼굴을 찡그리다; 눈살을 찌푸리다; n. 찡그림, 찌푸림
When someone frowns, their eyebrows become drawn together, because they are annoyed or puzzled.

★★ **fault** [fɔːlt] n. 잘못, 책임; 결점
If a bad or undesirable situation is your fault, you caused it or are responsible for it.

★★ **interrupt** [ìntərʌ́pt] v. (말·행동을) 방해하다; 중단시키다; 차단하다
If you interrupt someone who is speaking, you say or do something that causes them to stop.

★★ **confuse** [kənfjúːz] v. (사람을) 혼란시키다; 혼동하다 (confusing a. 혼란스러운)
If something is confusing, it is not easy to understand because it is complicated or not well organized or explained.

복습 **real live** [ríːəl làiv] a. 실물의, 진짜의
You use real live to say that someone or something is present or exists, when you want to indicate that you think this is exciting and unusual or unexpected.

★★ **plain** [plein] a. 평범한; 분명한; 솔직한; ad. 분명히, 완전히
If you describe someone or something as plain, you emphasize that they are very ordinary, not special in any way.

복습 **nanna** [nǽnə] n. 할머니; 유모
Some people refer to their grandmother as their nan or nanna.

★ **couch** [kauʧ] n. 소파, 긴 의자
A couch is a long, comfortable seat for two or three people.

bum [bʌm] n. 게으름뱅이, 쓸모없는 사람; v. ~를 화나게 하다
If someone refers to another person as a bum, they think that person is worthless or irresponsible.

★ **bunch** [bʌnʧ] n. (양·수가) 많음; 다발, 송이, 묶음
A bunch of things is a number of things, especially a large number.

복습 **cry-baby** [krái-bèibi] n. 울보
If you call a child a cry-baby, you mean that the child cries a lot for no good reason.

parking lot [pá:rkiŋ lat] n. 주차장
A parking lot is an area of ground where people can leave their cars.

복습 **speedy** [spí:di] a. 빠른, 신속한
A speedy process, event, or action happens or is done very quickly.

복습 **hug** [hʌg] v. 껴안다, 포옹하다; n. 포옹
When you hug someone, you put your arms around them and hold them tightly, for example because you like them or are pleased to see them.

★ **blanket** [blǽŋkit] n. 담요, 모포; v. (완전히) 뒤덮다
A blanket is a large square or rectangular piece of thick cloth, especially one which you put on a bed to keep you warm.

복습 **teeny** [tí:ni] a. 아주 작은
If you describe something as teeny, you are emphasizing that it is very small.

pinkish [píŋkiʃ] a. 분홍색을 띤
Something pinkish is similar to pink or slightly pink in color.

복습 **except** [iksépt] conj. ~이지만, ~라는 점만 제외하면; prep. ~ 외에는; v. 제외하다
You can use except to introduce a statement that makes what you have just said seem less true or less possible.

fuzzy [fʌ́zi] a. 솜털이 보송보송한; 흐릿한, 어렴풋한
If something is fuzzy, it has a covering that feels soft and like fur.

복습 **polite** [pəláit] a. 예의 바른, 공손한, 정중한; 예의상의
Someone who is polite has good manners and behaves in a way that is socially correct and not rude to other people.

★★★ **lift** [lift] v. 들어 올리다, 올라가다; n. (차 등을) 태워 주기
If you lift something, you move it to another position, especially upward.

복습 **peep** [pi:p] v. 살짝 보다, 훔쳐보다; 살짝 보이다; n. 훔쳐보기, 살짝 봄
If you peep or peep at something, you take a quick look at it, often secretly and quietly.

1장 깜짝 놀랄 일

내 이름은 주니 B. 존스(Junie B. Jones) 입니다. B는 비어트리스(Beatrice)를 나타냅니다. 하지만 나는 비어트리스라는 이름을 좋아하지 않습니다. 나는 그냥 B를 좋아할 뿐이고 그게 다입니다. B는 또한, 다른 말을 나타내기도 합니다.

B는 아-기(B-A-B-Y)를 나타냅니다.

나는 아직 학교 유치부에 다닙니다. 하지만 나는 벌써 아-기의 철자를 쓸 줄 압니다. 그건 우리 엄마가 자신이 그런 것 중 하나를 가질 거라고 나에게 말해 주었기 때문입니다.

엄마와 아빠는 어느 날 밤 저녁 식사 자리에서 나에게 그것에 대해 말해 주었습니다. 그날 저녁에 우리는 토마토 스튜를 먹었는데—그것은 내가 정말 싫어하는 것입니다.

"아빠랑 엄마가 너에게 알려 줄 깜짝 놀랄 일이 있어, 주니 B." 엄마가 말했습니다.

그리고 그래서 그때 나는 마음속으로 아주 행복해졌습니다. 왜냐하면 내가 나의 역겨운 토마토 스튜를 다 먹지 않아도 될 것 같았거든요.

그리고 또 가끔 깜짝 놀랄 일은 선물을 의미하기도 하죠! 그리고 선물은 내가 세상에서 가장 제일 좋아하는 것이에요!

나는 내 의자 위에서 폴짝폴짝 뛰었습니다.

"그게 뭔데요? 그건 다 포장되어 있나요? 난 그게 안 보여요." 나는 매우 흥분해서 말했습니다.

그런 다음 나는 식탁 밑을 보았습니다. 왜냐하면 깜짝 놀랄 일이 그것 위에 빨간 리본을 단 채 그 아래 숨어 있을 수도 있으니까요.

엄마와 아빠는 서로를 향해 미소 지었습니다. 그러고 나서 엄마는 내 손을 잡았습니다.

"주니 B., 너에게 아기 남동생이나 아기 여동생이 있으면 어떨 것 같니?" 엄마가 말했습니다.

나는 내 어깨를 위아래로 으쓱했습니다.

"모르겠어요. 글쎄요." 나는 엄마에게 말했습니다.

그러고 나서 나는 의자 밑을 보았습니다.

"그거 아세요?" 내가 말했습니다. "저는 그 바보 같은 선물을 어디에서도 찾을 수가 없어요."

엄마는 나를 똑바로 앉혔습니다. 그런 다음 엄마와 아빠는 아기에 대해 좀 더 이야기했습니다.

"아기는 네 아기이기도 할 거야, 주니 B." 아빠가 말했습니다. "생각해 보렴.

너에게 같이 놀 수 있는 너만의 남동생이나 여동생이 생기는 거야. 재미있지 않겠니?"

나는 또다시 내 어깨를 위아래로 으쓱했습니다. "모르겠어요. 글쎄요." 내가 말했습니다.

그런 다음 나는 의자에서 내려와서 거실로 뛰어 들어갔습니다.

"안 좋은 소식이 있어, 친구들!" 나는 아주 크게 소리 질렀습니다. **"역시나, 이 멍청한 방 안에도 선물은 없다는 거야!"**

엄마와 아빠가 거실로 들어왔습니다. 그들은 더 이상 그렇게 웃는 얼굴로 보이지 않았습니다.

아빠가 크게 숨을 쉬었습니다. "선물은 없단다, 주니 B." 그가 말했습니다. "우리가 선물이 있다고 말한 적은 없어. 우리는 *깜짝 놀랄 일*이 있다고 했단다. 기억하지?"

그러고 나서 엄마는 내 옆에 앉았습니다. "깜짝 놀랄 일은 엄마가 *아기*를 낳을 거라는 거야, 주니 B. 몇 달 후면 너에게 아기 남동생이나 아기 여동생이 생길 거란다. 이제 내가 무슨 말을 하는지 알겠니?"

바로 그때 나는 팔짱을 끼고 짜증 난 표정을 지었습니다. 왜냐면 갑자기 나는 그 말을 이해했기 때문이고, 그래서 그랬습니다.

"엄마가 나에게 망할 선물을 주지 않는다는 거잖아요, 그렇죠?" 나는 몹시 으르렁거리며 말했습니다.

엄마는 나에게 화가 나 보였습니다. "내가 졌다!" 그녀가 말했습니다. 그러고 나서 그녀는 부엌으로 돌아갔습니다.

아빠는 내가 엄마에게 사가('pology)를 해야 한다고 말했습니다.

사가는 내가 *죄송해요*라고 말해야 하는 때를 말합니다.

"네, 그런데 엄마도 나에게 사가해야 해요, 마찬가지로 말이죠." 내가 말했습니다. "왜냐하면 아기는 아주 좋은 깜짝 놀랄 일이 아니기 때문이에요."

나는 주름진 코를 만들어 보였습니다. "아기들은 냄새가 지독해요." 내가 설명했습니다. "나는 내 친구 그레이스(Grace)의 집에서 한번 맡아 봤어요. 아기는 몸 앞쪽에 토를 조금 묻히고 있었어요. 그리고 그래서 나는 내 코를 쥐고 소리를 질렀죠. **'으휴! 완전 방귀 폭탄이잖아!'** 그리고 그다음에 그 그레이스는 나에게 집에 가라고 했어요."

내가 이야기를 끝내자, 아빠는 부엌으로 들어가서 엄마와 이야기했습니다.

그러고 나서 엄마는 그 안에서 나를 불렀습니다. 그리고 그녀는 만약 아기에게서 방귀 폭탄 같은 냄새가 난다면,

나에게 나만의 방향제를 사 줄 것이라고 말했습니다. 그리고 내가 직접 그 방향제를 뿌려도 된다고 말했어요.

냄새나는 아기에게는 빼고 말이죠.

"캐롤라이나(Carolina) 소나무 숲처럼 상쾌한 향이 나는 방향제를 가지고 싶어요." 내가 말했습니다.

그런 다음 나와 엄마는 포옹했습니다. 그리고 나는 다시 식탁에 앉았습니다. 그리고 나는 저녁 먹는 것을 마쳤습니다.

나의 역겨운 토마토 스튜는 빼고요.

그리고 그거 아세요?

그건 바로, 디저트가 없었다는 거예요.

2장 멍청한 아기방

엄마와 아빠는 새로 태어날 아기를 위해 방을 하나 마련했습니다. 그것은 아기방(nursery)이라고 불립니다. 하지만 나는 그 이유를 모르겠습니다. 왜냐하면 아기는 간호사(nurse)가 아니니까요, 당연히 말이에요.

그 아기방은 원래 손님방이었습니다. 그곳에서 우리의 모든 손님들이 자곤 했습니다. 하지만 우리는 한 번도 손님이 많았던 적이 없었습니다.

그리고 그래서 이제부터 우리가 손님을 받게 되면, 그들은 탁자 같은 곳 위에서 자야 할 것입니다.

아기방에는 새 물건들이 있습니다. 그것은 바로 엄마와 아빠가 갓난아기용 물건 가게에 쇼핑을 다녀왔기 때문입니다.

그들은 초록색과 노란색 손잡이가 달린 갓난아기용 서랍장을 샀습니다. 그리고 전등갓에 기린이 그려진 갓난아기용 전등도요. 그리고 또, 아기가 우는데 아기를 조용히 시킬 수 없을 때를 위한 새 흔들의자도요.

그리고 또, 갓난아기용 침대도 있습니다.

아기 침대는 옆쪽에 창살이 있는 침대입니다. 그것은 마치 동물원에 있는 우리와 비슷합니다. 하지만 아기 침대에서는, 창살 사이로 손을 집어넣을 수 있습니다. 그래도 아기가 여러분을 안으로 끌어당겨 죽이지는 않을 테니까요.

그리고 아기방에 또 뭐가 있는지 아세요? 그건 바로, 벽지입니다! 정글 종류랍니다. 코끼리, 그리고 사자, 그리고 크고 뚱뚱한 하마-라든가-뭐라든가의 그림이 그려져 있습니다.

그리고 또, 원숭이도 있습니다! 그것은 내가 세상에서 가장 제일 좋아하는 정글 친구예요!

엄마와 아빠는 함께 벽지에 풀을 발

랐습니다.

나와 나의 개 티클(Tickle)은 그들을 보고 있었습니다.

"이 벽지가 여기에서 아주 귀여워 보여요." 내가 부모님에게 말했습니다. "내 생각엔, 똑같이, 내 방에도 이 벽지가 좀 있었으면 좋겠어요. 괜찮을까요?" 내가 말했습니다. "그래도 돼요? 그래도 돼요?"

"두고 보자꾸나." 아빠가 말했습니다.

*두고 보자꾸나*는 안 돼의 다른 말입니다.

"네, 하지만 그건 공평하지 않아요." 내가 말했습니다. "왜냐면 아기는 온통 새 물건을 갖고 나는 온통 낡은 물건만 가지니까요."

"불쌍한 주니 B." 엄마가 아주 장난치듯 말했습니다.

그러고 나서 엄마는 몸을 숙여 나를 안으려고 했습니다. 하지만 그녀는 그렇게 잘 안아 줄 수 없었습니다. 엄마의 크고 뚱뚱한 배 때문이었는데—그곳은 바로 멍청한 아기가 있는 곳입니다.

"나는 이 바보 같은 아기를 좋아할 것 같지 않아요." 내가 말했습니다.

엄마는 나를 껴안는 것을 멈췄습니다.

"그런 말 하지 마, 주니 B. 넌 당연히 좋아할 거야." 엄마가 말했습니다.

"나는 당연히 안 좋아할 거예요." 나는 대꾸했습니다. "왜냐하면 아기는 내가 엄마를 아주 잘 안아 주도록 내버려 두지 않을 테니까요. 그리고 어쨌든, 나는 아기의 멍청하고 바보 같은 이름도 몰라요."

그러자 엄마는 새로 산 흔들의자에 앉았습니다. 그리고 엄마는 나를 그녀의 무릎 위에 앉히려고 했습니다. 하지만 나는 잘 맞지 않았습니다. 그래서 엄마는 그냥 내 손을 잡았습니다.

"그건 아빠와 엄마가 아직 아기 이름을 정하지 않았기 때문이야." 엄마가 설명했습니다. "우리는 약간 색다른 이름을 짓고 싶어. 있잖니, 주니 B. 존스처럼 뭔가 귀여운 이름으로. 사람들이 기억할 이름 말이야."

그리고 그래서 나는 아주 열심히 생각하고 또 생각했습니다. 그리고 그런 다음 나는 아주 큰 소리로 손뼉을 쳤습니다.

"엄마! 내가 하나 알아요!" 나는 매우 신나서 말했습니다. "바로 우리 학교의 구내식당 아주머니예요. 그리고 아주머니의 이름은 거츠먼 아주머니(Mrs. Gutzman)예요!"

엄마는 살짝 얼굴을 찌푸렸습니다. 그리고 그래서 아마 엄마가 내 얘기를 못 들은 것 같았어요, 내 생각에는요.

"거츠먼 아주머니요!" 내가 소리 질렀습니다. "그건 귀여운 이름이에요, 그렇지 않아요? 그리고 또, 내가 이름을 기억하기도 했고요! 심지어 나는 그 이름을 딱 한 번 들은 뒤였는데, 거츠먼 아주머니가 내 머리에 바로 꽂혔어요!"

엄마는 크게 숨을 쉬었습니다. "그래, 얘야. 하지만 나는 거츠먼 아주머니가 작은 아기에게 어울리는 이름인지는 모르겠구나."

그리고 그래서 그다음에 나는 얼굴을 찡그렸습니다. 그리고 나는 다시 생각하고 또 생각했습니다.

"꼬맹이(Teeny)는 어때요?" 내가 말했습니다. "꼬맹이가 좋을 것 같아요."

엄마가 미소 지었습니다. "글쎄, 아기가 어릴 때는 꼬맹이라는 이름도 귀여울 것 같아. 그런데 아기가 자라면 우리는 그 애를 뭐라고 불러야 할까?"

"큰 꼬맹이(Big Teeny)!" 나는 아주 행복하게 소리쳤습니다.

그러자 엄마가 말했습니다. "두고 보자꾸나."

그것은 큰 꼬맹이는 안 된다는 말이죠.

그런 다음, 나는 더 이상 그렇게 행복하지 않았습니다.

"아무튼 이 바보 같은 아기는 언제 여기 오는 거예요?" 내가 말했습니다.

엄마가 다시 얼굴을 찌푸렸습니다. "아기는 바보가 아니야, 주니 B." 엄마가 말했습니다. "그리고 아기는 정말 금방 여기에 올 거란다. 그러니까 엄마가 생각하기에는 네가 그 사실에 익숙해지기 시작하는 게 좋을 것 같아."

그러고 나서 엄마와 아빠는 다시 벽지를 붙이기 시작했습니다.

그리고 그래서 나는 초록색과 노란색 손잡이가 달린 갓난아기용 서랍장을 열었습니다. 그리고 나는 새로 태어날 아기의 옷들을 쳐다보았습니다.

아기 잠옷은 아주 자그마했습니다. 그리고 아기 양말은 심지어 내 엄지발가락에도 맞지 않았습니다.

"나는 이 아기의 대장이 될 거야." 나는 티클에게 말했습니다. "왜냐면 내가 제일 크니까, 그래서 그런 거지."

아빠는 나를 향해 탁 하고 자신의 손가락을 튕겼습니다. "그런 이야기는 그만하렴, 아가씨." 그가 말했습니다.

아가씨는 내가 꾸지람을 들을 때의 내 이름입니다.

그런 다음, 아빠와 엄마는 풀을 좀 더 가지러 부엌으로 갔습니다.

그리고 그래서 나는 복도를 내다보며 아빠가 떠났는지 확인했습니다.

"그래, 하지만 그래도 나는 아기의 대장이 될 거야." 나는 소곤거렸습니다.

하하. 그렇게 하고 말 거예요.

어제는 아주 멋진 일이 일어났습니다!

그리고 그것은 바로—내가 저녁으로 파이를 먹었다는 것이죠!

파이뿐이었고 그게 다입니다!

왜냐하면 우리 엄마가 아기를 낳으러 병원에 갔기 때문입니다. 그리고 아빠와 밀러 할머니(Grandma Miller)가 그녀와 함께 갔습니다.

그리고 그래서 나와 내 할아버지는 그의 집에 있어야 했습니다. 우리끼리만요. 그리고 아무도 우리를 돌봐 주지도 않았습니다!

그리고 그거 아세요? 할아버지는 집 안에서 진짜 시가(cigar)를 피웠습니다! 그리고 할머니가 이렇게 소리 지르지도 않았죠. "그거 가지고 밖으로 나가요, 프랭크(Frank)!"

그 후, 나의 할아버지는 나에게 어부바를 해 주었습니다.

그리고 그는 내가 밀러 할머니의 새로 산 모자도 써 보게 해 주었는데—기다란 갈색 깃털이 붙어 있는 것이었어요.

그리고 또, 나는 할머니의 빨간 하이힐을 신고 걷게 되었습니다.

하지만 그때 나는 부엌에서 넘어졌습니다. 그리고 그래서 나는 얼른 그것들을 벗어 버렸습니다.

"이런! 내가 이 멍청한 신발을 신다가는 머리를 깨뜨릴 수도 있겠어." 나는 아주 크게 말했습니다.

그 후에, 나는 넹장고('frigerator)를 열었습니다. 왜냐면 노느라 배가 고팠고, 그래서 그랬습니다.

"이것 봐요! 그거 알아요? 여기에 엄청 커다란 레몬 파이가 있어요, 프랭크!" 내가 소리 질렀습니다.

그리고 그래서 그런 다음 밀러 할아버지(Grampa Miller)는 레몬 파이 두 접시를 내왔습니다. 그리고 그 후 나와 할아버지는 저녁으로 그 엄청 커다란 레몬 파이를 먹었습니다!!

파이만 먹었고 그게 다입니다!!

그리고 우리는 꾸중을 듣지도 않을 것입니다! 왜냐면 우리는 할머니에게 고양이가 그것을 먹었다고 말할 것이기 때문입니다!

그리고 여기 아주 재미있는 일이 하나 더 있습니다. 내가 밀러 할아버지네 손님방에서 자게 된 것입니다!

우선 나는 발이 달린 내 잠옷을 입었습니다. 그리고 그다음에 나의 할아버지는 내가 새로 난 앞니를 닦는 것을 보았습니다. 그리고 그는 나를 커다란 손님 침대에 눕혔습니다.

"좋은 꿈 꾸렴, 주니 B." 그가 말했습니다.

하지만 그때 나는 살짝 겁이 났습니다.

"네. 근데 있잖아요, 할아버지." 내가 말했습니다. "이 커다란 방은 너무 어두워요. 그리고 그래서 여기에 숨어 있는 것들이 있을 것 같아요."

할아버지는 방 전체를 둘러보았습니다. 그리고 옷장 안도요.

"아니야. 여기에는 숨어 있는 것들이 없단다." 그가 말했습니다.

그런 다음 그는 나를 위해 복도 불을 켜 놓았습니다. 그래서 내 상상이 제멋대로 펼쳐지지 않도록 말이에요.

하지만 나는 그래도 잠을 푹 자지 못했습니다. 왜냐면 침 흘리는 누군가가 발톱을 드러내고 내 침대 밑에 있는 것 같았으니까요, 내 생각에 말이죠.

그리고 그래서 오늘 아침, 내 두 눈은 아주 처지는 느낌이었습니다.

하지만 바로 그때 나는 내 눈을 깨우는 무언가의 냄새를 맡았습니다.

그리고 그것의 이름은 맛있는 와플이었죠!

밀러 할아버지가 나를 위해 만들어 주었습니다! 그리고 그는 내가 스스로 시럽을 뿌리게 해 주었습니다. 그리고 그는 워! 워! 워! 하고 소리 지르지도 않았습니다.

그런 다음, 나와 할아버지는 학교에 갈 시간이 될 때까지 놀았습니다.

하지만 내가 출발하기 전에, 무엇보다도 가장 재미있는 일이 벌어졌습니다! 나의 밀러 할머니가 집에 온 것입니다!

그리고 할머니는 엄마가 아기를 낳았다고 말했습니다!

그리고 아기는 남자아이 종류였습니다!

그러고 나서 나와 할머니 그리고 할아버지는 모두 아주 큰 포옹을 했습니다!

그리고 밀러 할머니는 나를 들어 올렸습니다. 그리고 공중에서 나를 흔들었습니다.

"너는 곧바로 그 애를 사랑하게 될 거야, 주니 B.!" 그녀가 말했습니다. "새로 태어난 네 남동생은 내가 지금까지 본 것 중에 가장 귀여운 아기 원숭이란다!"

그러자 내 눈이 매우 커졌습니다. "그 애가요? 정말이에요?" 내가 말했습니다.

밀러 할머니는 나를 내려놓았습니다. 그리고 나서 그녀는 내 할아버지에게 말하기 시작했습니다.

"당신이 아기를 보면 알 거예요, 프랭크." 그녀가 말했습니다. "그 애는 작은 손가락과 발가락이 정말 길어요!"

나는 할머니의 원피스를 잡아당겼습니다. "얼마나 긴데요, 할머니?" 내가 말했습니다. "내 것보다 길어요?"

하지만 할머니는 그저 계속 말하기

만 했습니다.

"그리고 그 애 머리카락이요, 프랭크! 세상에! 숱 많고 검은 머리카락이 아주 아주 풍성해요!"

나는 할머니의 팔을 잡아당겼습니다. "왜요, 할머니? 왜 아기한테 머리카락이 있어요?" 나는 물었습니다. "난 작은 아기들은 대머리인 줄 알았는데요."

하지만 여전히, 할머니는 내 말에 대답하지 않았습니다.

"그리고 또, 녀석이 크기도 해요, 프랭크. 그 애는 병원에 있는 다른 어떤 아기들보다도 훨씬 커요. 그리고 당신은 녀석이 당신의 손가락을 얼마나 꽉 쥐는지 느껴봐야 해요, 당신이—"

바로 그때 나는 내 발을 아주 세게 굴렀습니다.

"저기요! 난 여기 밑에서도 대답을 듣고 싶다고요, 헬렌(Helen)! 그는 내 아기이기도 해요, 알잖아요!"

밀러 할머니는 나를 향해 얼굴을 찌푸렸습니다. 왜냐면 내 생각에, 내가 그녀를 헬렌이라고 부르면 안 되기 때문입니다.

"죄송해요." 나는 약간 조용하게 말했습니다.

그러자 밀러 할머니는 내 옆으로 몸을 숙였습니다. 그리고 그래서 나는 더 이상 소리 지를 필요가 없었습니다.

"나에게 사실을 말하고 있는 거죠, 할머니?" 내가 말했습니다. "내 남동생이 정말로 할머니가 지금까지 본 것 중에 가장 귀여운 아기 원숭이예요? 정말로 솔직하게 진짜로요?"

그러자 밀러 할머니는 나를 아주 꽉 안아 주었습니다.

"그럼, 꼬마 아가씨." 할머니가 내 귀에 속삭였습니다. "정말로 솔직하게 진짜로."

그 후에, 할머니는 나를 다시 들어 올렸습니다. 그리고 나와 할머니는 부엌 여기저기를 빙글빙글 돌면서 춤을 추었습니다.

4장 호피(Hoppy)와 러셀(Russell)

학교에서 나의 반은 9반(Room Nine)이라는 이름입니다.

나는 그곳에 가장 친한 친구들이 두 명 있습니다. 그중 한 명은 루실(Lucille)이라는 이름을 가졌습니다.

루실은 바로 정확히 내 옆에 앉습니다.

그녀는 빨간색 의자를 가지고 있습니다. 그리고 또 아주 반짝이는 작은 빨간색 손톱도요.

나와 가장 친한 다른 친구의 이름은 그레이스입니다.

나와 그 그레이스는 스쿨버스에서

같이 앉습니다. 하지만 오늘 우리는 그렇게 하지 않았습니다. 왜냐하면 오늘은 밀러 할아버지가 나를 태워다 주었기 때문입니다.

그러고 나서 그는 나와 함께 9반까지 걸어갔습니다. 그리고 그는 나의 선생님에게 손을 흔들었습니다.

그녀의 이름은 선생님(Mrs.)입니다.

또한, 선생님은 다른 이름도 가지고 있습니다. 하지만 나는 그냥 선생님이라는 이름을 좋아할 뿐이고 그게 다예요.

내가 처음으로 내 교실에 걸어 들어갔을 때, 루실은 그 그레이스의 새 신발을 보고 있었습니다. 그리고 그것들의 이름은 분홍색 하이 톱 운동화였습니다.

"야, 그레이스! 그 새 신발 너한테 정말 예쁘게 어울린다!" 내가 말했습니다.

하지만 그 멍청한 그레이스는 나에게 *고마워*라는 말조차 하지 않았습니다.

"그레이스는 너한테 화났어." 루실이 말했습니다. "그레이스가 그러는데 얘가 오늘 버스에 탔대. 그런데 네가 얘 자리를 맡아 주려고 거기 있지도 않았다는 거야. 그래서 그레이스는 어떤 기분 나쁜 애 옆에 앉아야 했대. 그렇지, 그레이스?"

그레이스는 자신의 고개를 위아래로 까닥거렸습니다.

"그래, 하지만 나도 어쩔 수 없었어, 그레이스." 내가 말했습니다. "그건 내가 밤새도록 밀러 할아버지 집에 있었기 때문이야. 그리고 그곳에는 버스가 없거든. 그리고 그래서 할아버지가 오늘 나를 여기로 태워 줘야 했어."

그런 다음 나는 그 그레이스의 손을 잡으려고 했습니다. 하지만 그녀는 재빨리 손을 뺐습니다.

"너 그것 정말 좋지 않은 행동이야, 그레이스." 내가 말했습니다. "그리고 그럼 이거 아니? 이제 나는 너에게 내 특별한 비밀을 말해 주지 않을 거야."

그때 그 그레이스는 나를 바보 멍청이라고 불렀습니다.

루실이 내 손을 잡았습니다. "*나*는 네가 바보 멍청이라고 생각하지 않아, 주니 B." 그녀가 말했습니다. "그리고 그러니까 너는 나에게 네 특별한 비밀을 말해도 돼. 그리고 나는 아무에게도 말하지 않을게. 심지어 그레이스에게도 말하지 않을 거야."

그때 그 그레이스가 루실의 다리를 걷어찼습니다.

그리고 그래서 루실은 그녀를 밀어 넘어뜨렸습니다.

그리고 선생님이 와서 그들을 서로에게서 떼어 놓아야 했습니다.

나는 아주 공손하게 손을 들었습니다. "저는 상관없는 일이에요." 나는 선생님에게 말했습니다.

그 후에, 우리는 앉아서 공부를 조금 해야 했습니다. 그것은 숫자를 또박또박 쓰기라고 불립니다. 하지만 나는 내 일을 그렇게 잘할 수 없었습니다. 왜냐하면 루실이 계속해서 나에게 말을 걸었기 때문이고, 그래서 그렇습니다.

"어서, 주니 B." 그녀가 소곤거리는 목소리로 말했습니다. "나에게 너의 특별한 비밀을 말해 줘. 나는 말 안 할게. 약속해."

"그래, 하지만 나는 그럴 수 없어, 루실." 내가 말했습니다. "왜냐면 옆 사람에게 이야기 금지잖아, 기억나지?"

그때 선생님이 나를 향해 탁 하고 손가락을 튕겼습니다.

"봤지, 루실? 내가 옆 사람에게 이야기 금지라고 했잖아!" 나는 소리 질렀습니다. **"방금 내가 탁 하는 소리를 들었다고!"**

바로 그때 짐(Jim)이라는 이름의 남자아이가 나에게 말했습니다. "쉿."

"너나 조용히 해, 이 멍청한 짐." 내가 대꾸했습니다.

그 후, 선생님은 내가 내 공부를 끝낼 때까지 내 옆에 서 있었습니다. 그런 다음 나는 모두 끝냈고 그녀는 그것을 가지고 갔습니다.

그것은 나의 마음속을 행복하게 했습니다. 왜냐하면 공부를 한 다음에 무엇이 오는 줄 아세요? 바로 그건, 아주 재미있는 것이에요!

그리고 그것의 이름은 발표 시간(Show and Tell)입니다.

선생님은 자신의 책상 옆에 섰습니다. "오늘 반 친구들과 나눌 무언가 흥미로운 것이 있는 사람?" 그녀가 말했습니다.

그러자 나의 심장이 엄청나게 쿵쿵거렸습니다. 왜냐하면 나는 세상에서 가장 특별한 비밀을 가지고 있었기 때문입니다!

나는 손을 공중으로 높이 들었습니다.

"오오오오오! 오오오오오!" 나는 정말 큰 소리로 소리 질렀습니다. **"저요! 저요! 저요!"**

선생님은 나를 향해 자신의 고개를 가로저었습니다. 왜냐하면 나는 오오오오오, 오오오오오, 저요, 저요, 저요라고 하면 안 되기 때문입니다.

그녀는 윌리엄(William)의 이름을 불렀습니다. 그는 우리 반의 울보 녀석입니다. 나는 그를 때려눕힐 수 있어요, 내 생각에는요.

"윌리엄?" 선생님이 말했습니다. "네가 아주 공손하게 손을 들었으니까, 네가 먼저 하도록 하렴."

그리고 그래서 그때 윌리엄이 교실 앞으로 종이 가방을 가지고 나왔습니다. 그리고 그는 죽은 귀뚜라미 두 마리가 들어 있는 병을 꺼냈습니다.

다만 윌리엄은 그것들이 죽었다는 것을 몰랐을 뿐입니다. 그는 그냥 그것들이 자고 있다고 생각했습니다.

"뛰어 봐, 호피! 뛰어 봐, 러셀!" 윌리엄이 말했습니다.

그러고 나서 그는 유리병을 두드렸습니다.

"야! 거기 일어나라고!" 그가 말했습니다.

그런 후에, 윌리엄은 병을 사방으로 흔들기 시작했습니다. 그리고 그는 멈추지 않았습니다.

"**일어나라고, 내가 말했잖아!**" 그가 소리쳤습니다.

그때 호피와 러셀이 온통 부서지기 시작했습니다. 그리고 선생님은 그 병을 빼앗아야 했습니다.

바로 그때 윌리엄이 울기 시작했습니다. 그리고 그는 보건실로 가서 누워 있어야 했습니다.

그리고 그래서 그때 나는 다시 손을 공중으로 아주 높이 들었습니다.

왜 그런지 아세요? 내 발표가 죽은 귀뚜라미 두 마리보다 *훨씬* 더 나았기 때문이죠!

5장 원숭이 소동

선생님이 내 이름을 불렀습니다.

"주니 B.? 네가 다음으로 발표하겠니?" 그녀가 물었습니다.

그때 나는 곧바로 자리에서 벌떡 일어났습니다. 그리고 나는 교실 앞으로 아주 잽싸게 뛰어갔습니다.

"이거 아니?" 나는 무척 흥분해서 말했습니다. "어젯밤에 우리 엄마가 아기를 낳았어! 그리고 그건 남자아이 종류야!"

선생님은 박수를 쳤습니다.

"주니 B. 존스에게 남동생이 생겼대요, 여러분!" 그녀가 말했습니다. "근사하지 않나요?"

그러자 마찬가지로, 9반 친구들 모두가 박수를 쳤습니다.

"그래, 하지만 너희는 아직 가장 멋진 부분을 듣지도 못했어!" 내가 아주 큰 소리로 말했습니다. "왜냐하면 또 그거 알아? 그 애는 **원숭이**야! 바로 그거야! 새로 태어난 내 남동생은 진짜, 살아 있는, 아기 **원숭이**야!!!"

선생님은 얼굴에 이상한 표정을 지었습니다. 그리고 그녀는 그녀의 눈을 아주 가늘게 떴습니다. 그리고 그래서 아마 내 생각에는, 선생님이 내 말을 듣지 못했거나 그랬던 것 같았습니다.

"**나는 나에게 원숭이 남동생이 생**

겼다고 말했어요!" 나는 훨씬 더 크게 소리쳤습니다.

그러자 못된 짐 그 녀석이 자기 책상에서 바로 벌떡 일어났습니다. 그리고 그는 소리 질렀습니다. "거짓말쟁이, 거짓말쟁이, 바지에 불붙었대요!"

"아니 바지에 불 안 붙었거든, 이 바보 같은 짐!" 내가 대꾸했습니다. "나는 정말로 원숭이 남동생이 있어! 네가 내 말을 못 믿겠으면 우리 밀러 할머니한테 물어봐!"

선생님은 그녀의 두 눈썹을 자신의 머리 위로 높이 치켜 올렸습니다.

"너희 할머니가 네 남동생이 원숭이라고 말하셨다고?" 그녀가 나에게 물었습니다.

"네!" 내가 말했습니다. "할머니는 그 애가 기다란 손가락과 발가락을 가지고 있다고 했어요. 그리고 그 애의 온몸에 검은 털도 많다고 했어요!"

그 후에, 선생님은 계속해서 나를 쳐다보고 또 쳐다보았습니다. 그리고 나서 그녀는 이제 내가 앉을 시간이라고 말했습니다.

"네, 하지만 나는 내 원숭이 남동생에 대해 친구들에게 말하는 게 아직 끝나지 않았어요." 나는 설명했습니다.

"왜냐면 또 이거 알아? 그 애의 방 벽지에는 정글 친구들의 그림이 있어. 그리고 그 애의 침대 양쪽에는 창살이 있고. 하지만 내가 그 애에게 사람을 물거나 죽이면 안 된다고 가르쳐 줄 거야."

그때 리카도(Ricardo)라는 이름의—얼굴에 귀여운 주근깨들이 있는—남자아이가 나에게 말했습니다. "원숭이들은 멋지지."

"맞아 원숭이들은 멋져, 리카도." 내가 말했습니다. "그리고 또 이거 아니? 아마 내가 애완동물의 날(Pet Day)에 그 애를 학교로 데려올 수도 있을 거야."

그러자 리카도는 나를 향해 미소 지었습니다. 그리고 그래서 내 생각에는, 그 애가 내 남자친구여도 될 것 같아요. 8반(Room Eight)에 벌써 나를 무척 좋아하는 남자아이가 있긴 하지만요.

바로 그때, 선생님이 일어나서 나를 가리켰습니다.

"이제 됐어, 주니 B." 그녀가 말했습니다. "이제 너는 자리에 앉도록 해. 너하고 선생님은 이 원숭이 소동에 관해 나중에 이야기할 거야."

그리고 그래서 그 말이 나를 킥킥 웃게 했습니다. 왜냐하면 내 생각에, 원숭이 소동은 웃긴 말이기 때문입니다.

그리고 나서 나는 내 새로운 남자친구, 리카도에게 손을 흔들어 인사했습니다.

그리고 나는 내 자리로 깡총깡총 뛰

어서 돌아갔습니다.

6장 가장 친한 친구들

쉬는 시간은 내가 제일 잘하는 과목입니다. 나는 학교 유치부에서의 첫째 주에 그것을 알게 되었습니다.

쉬는 시간은 여러분이 밖에 나가는 때입니다. 그리고 여러분은 기운을 좀 뺍니다.

그러고 나서 들어오면, 여러분은 더 잘 가만히 앉아 있을 수 있습니다. 그리고 여러분은 바지에 개미가 들어 있는 것처럼 꼼지락거리지도 않게 됩니다.

쉬는 시간에, 나와 루실 그리고 그 그레이스는 함께 말처럼 뛰어다니며 놉니다.

나는 밤톨이(Brownie)입니다. 루실은 까망이(Blackie)이지요. 그리고 그 그레이스는 노랑이(Yellowie)입니다.

"나는 밤톨이다!" 나는 밖으로 나가자마자 소리 질렀습니다.

"나는 오늘 말 놀이를 하고 싶지 않아." 루실이 말했습니다. "나는 네 원숭이 남동생에 대해 좀 더 알고 싶어."

"나도 마찬가지야." 그 그레이스가 말했습니다.

그러자 루실은 그 그레이스를 밀쳐냈습니다. 그리고 그녀는 내 귀에 비밀을 소곤거렸습니다.

"만약 내가 그 애를 처음으로 보는 사람이 되게 해 주면, 나는 내 새 펜던트 목걸이를 네가 하게 해 줄게." 그녀가 말했습니다.

"그래. 그런데 그거 아니, 루실?" 내가 말했습니다. "나는 바보 같은 펜던트가 뭔지도 몰라."

그리고 그래서 그때 루실은 나에게 자기 펜던트를 보여 주었습니다. 그것은 목걸이 줄에 달린 작은 금색 하트였습니다.

"예쁘지 않니?" 그녀가 말했습니다. "우리 할머니가 내 생일에 나에게 이것을 주셨어."

그러고 나서 그녀는 그 작은 하트를 열었습니다. 그리고 그것 안에는 작고 조그마한 사진 한 장이 있었습니다!

"이야! 그 안에 조그만 머리가 있네!" 나는 매우 흥분해서 말했습니다.

"맞아." 루실이 말했습니다. "그건 우리 할머니야. 할머니가 보이니?"

나는 눈을 가늘게 뜨고 그 조그만 사진을 아주 열심히 보았습니다.

"너희 할머니는 정말 조그맣구나, 루실." 내가 말했습니다.

그 후에, 루실은 펜던트를 닫았습니다. 그리고 그녀는 그것을 나에게 주었습니다.

"이제 내가 너의 가장 친한 친구야,

그렇지, 주니 B.?" 그녀가 말했습니다. "그리고 그러니까 내가 너의 원숭이 남동생을 볼 첫 번째 사람이 될 수 있는 거지!"

바로 그때, 그 그레이스가 아주 세게 자신의 발을 굴렀습니다.

"아니 넌 그럴 수 없어, 루실!" 그녀가 소리 질렀습니다. "*내*가 주니 B.의 가장 친한 친구라고! 왜냐면 나랑 주니 B.는 버스를 같이 타거든. 그리고 그래서 내가 그녀의 원숭이 남동생을 먼저 봐야 하는 거야. 그렇지, 주니 B.? 그렇지? 그렇지?"

나는 위아래로 내 어깨를 으쓱거렸습니다.

"모르겠어, 그레이스." 내가 말했습니다. "왜냐면 루실이 방금 나에게 이 조그만 할머니가 있는 목걸이를 줬거든. 그리고 그래서 그건 그녀가 먼저 봐야 한다는 말인 거지, 내 생각에 말이야."

그 그레이스는 다시 자신의 발을 굴렀습니다. 그녀는 나에게 화난 얼굴을 했습니다.

"첫!" 그녀가 말했습니다.

그런데 바로 그때 나에게 좋은 생각이 떠올랐습니다!

"얘! 그거 아니, 그레이스?" 나는 몹시 흥분해서 말했습니다. "루실이 나에게 무언가 예쁜 것을 줬으니까, 마찬가지로, 이제 너도 나에게 무언가 예쁜 것을 주면 돼! 그리고 그러면 내가 아주 공평한 거지, 내 생각에는 말이야!"

그러자 그 그레이스는 미소 짓기 시작했습니다. 그리고 그녀는 자신의 반짝거리는 새 반지를 뺐습니다.

"여기 있어!" 그레이스가 말했습니다. "내가 오늘 아침에 시리얼에서 이걸 꺼냈어! 보석이 얼마나 빛나는지 보여? 그건 그게 진짜 진품인 가짜 플라스틱 다이아몬드이기 때문이야."

그러고 나서 그녀는 그것에 입김을 좀 불었습니다. 그리고 그녀는 나를 위해 자기 소매로 그걸 반짝거리게 했습니다.

"오오오오오." 내가 말했습니다. "나 이거 정말 마음에 든다, 그레이스."

"그럴 줄 알았어." 그녀가 말했습니다. "그리고 그러면 이제 내가 먼저 네 원숭이 남동생을 보게 되는 거야. 그렇지, 주니 B.? 그렇지?"

그 후 나는 조금 생각을 해야 했습니다.

"그래, 그런데 문제가 있어, 그레이스." 내가 말했습니다. "지금 나는 너에게서 하나를 받고 루실에게서 하나를 받았어. 그리고 그러면 이제 동점이야."

그러자 루실이 재빨리 스코티시 테리어(Scottie dog) 그림이 있는 그녀의 빨간 스웨터를 벗었습니다. 그리고 그녀는 그것을 내 허리에 둘러 주었습니다.

"여기!" 그녀가 말했습니다. "이제 나는 너에게 두 개를 준 거야! 그리고 그러니까 내가 계속 일등이라는 말이지."

"오 아니야 너 일등 아니거든!" 그 그레이스가 소리 질렀습니다. "왜냐하면 나는 주니 B.에게 오늘 쓸 내 간식 쿠폰을 줄 거니까. 그리고 그러면 그녀는 내 쿠키와 우유를 먹을 수 있어!"

"훌륭한 생각이야, 그레이스!" 내가 말했습니다.

그러고 나서 나와 그녀는 하이파이브를 했습니다.

"아 그래?" 루실이 말했습니다. "글쎄, 그러면, 나도 주니 B.에게 *내* 간식 쿠폰을 줄 거야, 똑같이! 그리고 그러면 내가 여전히 일등이라고!"

그 후 그레이스는 자신의 몸을 샅샅이 살펴보았습니다.

"하지만 그건 공평하지 않아." 그녀가 말했습니다. "왜냐하면 나는 주니 B.에게 줄 만한 다른 게 없다고."

그리고 그래서 나도 마찬가지로, 그녀를 샅샅이 살펴보았습니다. 그리고 그런 다음 나는 다시 폴짝폴짝 뛰었습니다.

"아니야 넌 가지고 있어, 그레이스!" 내가 말했습니다. "너 역시 나에게 줄 만한 다른 게 있어! 그리고 그것의 이름은 너의 새 분홍색 하이 톱 운동화야!"

그 그레이스는 자신의 발을 쳐다보았습니다. 그녀는 무척 슬퍼 보였습니다.

"그래, 그렇지만 내가 이걸 신은 건 이번이 처음인걸." 그녀는 아주 조용하게 말했습니다.

그리고 그래서 나는 그녀의 기분이 나아지도록 그녀를 토닥거렸습니다.

"나도 알아, 그레이스." 나는 상냥하게 설명했습니다. "하지만 네가 나에게 신발을 주지 않으면, 너는 내 원숭이 남동생을 볼 수 없을 거야."

그리고 그래서 그다음에 나와 그 그레이스는 잔디 위에 앉았습니다. 그리고 그녀는 자신의 새 분홍색 신발을 벗었습니다. 그리고 그녀는 그것들을 나에게 주었습니다.

"고마워, 그레이스." 나는 예의 바르게 말했습니다.

그런 다음 나는 일어났습니다.

"좋아. 네 차례야." 나는 루실에게 말했습니다.

하지만 내게는 정말 아쉬운 일이 일어났습니다. 왜냐면 바로 그때 멍청한 종이 울렸기 때문입니다.

7장 몇 가지 학교에서 쓰는 말

나는 나의 새 물건들을 걸치고 9반으

로 돌아왔습니다.

그것들은 나에게 아주 예쁘게 어울리는 듯이 보였습니다. 나의 새 분홍색 하이 톱 운동화가 너무 크기는 했지만요. 그리고 내 발은 그 안에서 여기저기로 잔뜩 미끄러지고 있었습니다.

내가 앉기 전에 나는 루실의 빨간 의자를 보았습니다. 그러고 나서 나는 그녀를 톡톡 쳤습니다.

"미안한데, 루실." 내가 말했습니다. "빨강은 내가 가장 좋아하는 색이거든. 그리고 그래서 나는 너의 그 의자가 갖고 싶은 것 같아, 내 생각에는."

루실은 나에게 아주 화가 난 표정을 지어 보였습니다. "그렇지만 빨강은 내가 가장 좋아하는 색이기도 해, 너처럼, 주니 B."

나는 그녀를 토닥거렸습니다. "맞아, 루실." 나는 다정하게 말했습니다. "하지만 너는 그래도 나에게 그걸 줘야 해. 그게 규칙이잖아."

그래서 그녀는 그렇게 했습니다.

"이제 내가 확실히 일등이야, 그렇지 않니?" 그녀가 물었습니다.

나는 내 어깨를 위아래로 으쓱거렸습니다. "나도 모르겠어, 루실." 내가 말했습니다. "그 그레이스가 자기 지갑에 돈이 좀 있을 거라고 했거든."

그 후에, 선생님은 도화지를 나누어 주었습니다. 그리고 우리는 게시판에 붙일 단풍잎을 오려 냈습니다.

*추계(autumn)*는 가을(fall)이라는 뜻의 학교에서 쓰는 말입니다.

우리는 우리의 나뭇잎에 빛나는 반짝이를 뿌렸습니다.

또, 나는 내 머리카락에도 반짝이를 뿌렸습니다. 그리고 나는 내 눈썹에도 반짝이를 조금 발랐습니다.

그러자 선생님은 내 빛나는 반짝이 병을 압수했습니다.

*압수하다*는 손에서 곧바로 그것을 확 잡아챘다는 뜻으로 학교에서 쓰는 말입니다.

바로 그때, 거츠먼 아주머니가 문을 두드렸습니다. 그리고 그녀는 우리의 우유와 쿠키를 가지고 교실로 들어왔습니다.

"만세! 거츠먼 아주머니 만세!" 나는 그녀를 향해 소리쳤습니다. "맞혀 볼래요, 거츠먼 아주머니? 나는 오늘 간식을 세 개 먹어요! 보이죠? 내가 간식 쿠폰을 세 장이나 가지고 있어요!"

선생님이 내 의자로 걸어왔습니다. 그녀는 나를 빤히 내려다보았습니다.

"너 어떻게 쿠폰 두 장을 더 얻은 거니, 주니 B.?" 그녀가 물었습니다. "너 운동장에서 그걸 찾은 거니?"

그러더니 그녀는 내 추가 쿠폰 두 장을 가져갔습니다. 그리고 그녀는 그것들을 공중으로 높이 들어 올렸습니다.

"오늘 자기 간식 쿠폰을 잃어버린 사람이 있나요?" 그녀는 반 아이들에게 말했습니다.

"없어요!" 나는 소리 질렀습니다. "그것들은 제 쿠폰이에요! 루실과 그레이스가 저에게 그것들을 준 거란 말이에요!"

선생님은 그녀의 두 눈썹을 치켜올렸습니다. "루실? 네가 오늘 주니 B.에게 네 간식 쿠폰을 주었니?" 그녀가 물었습니다.

"네." 루실이 말했습니다. "그건 그 애가 그렇게 하도록 나에게 시켰기 때문이에요."

"아니야, 나 안 그랬어, 이 멍청이 루실!" 내가 말했습니다. "나는 너에게 시키지 않았어!"

선생님은 나에게 말했습니다. "조용히 하렴."

그녀는 팔짱을 꼈습니다. "그레이스? 주니 B.에게 네 간식 쿠폰을 주었니, 너도?"

그러자 그 그레이스는 울기 시작했습니다. 왜냐하면 그녀는 자신이 꾸지람을 듣는다고 생각했기 때문입니다.

선생님은 자신의 발을 톡톡 굴렀습니다. "그레이스, 와서 네 간식 쿠폰을 가져가렴." 그녀가 말했습니다.

그리고 그래서 그때 그 그레이스는 양말만 신은 채로 내 책상으로 걸어왔습니다.

그리고 선생님은 눈을 가늘게 뜨고 그레이스의 발을 쳐다보았습니다.

"네 신발은 어디 있니, 그레이스?" 그녀가 물었습니다.

그때 짜증 나는 울보 그레이스가 훨씬 더 심하게 울기 시작했습니다. 그리고 그녀는 자신의 신발을 가리켰습니다.

선생님은 내 책상 아래를 흘끗 보았습니다.

"주니 B. 존스!" 그녀가 소리 질렀습니다. "왜 네가 그레이스의 신발을 신고 있는 거니?"

선생님의 목소리는 무시무시하게 들렸습니다.

"왜냐하면." 나는 약간 겁에 질려서 말했습니다.

"왜냐하면 왜?" 선생님이 말했습니다.

"왜냐하면 그게 규칙이라서요." 나는 설명했습니다.

그러자 선생님은 내 귀 쪽으로 아주 가까이 몸을 숙였습니다. "무슨 규칙?"

"누가 내 원숭이 남동생을 처음으로 보는 사람이 될지 정하는 규칙이요." 내가 말했습니다.

선생님은 그녀의 머리 저 뒤로 눈을 굴렸습니다.

"다시 네 신발을 신으렴. 그리고 나를 따라오렴, 꼬마 아가씨." 그녀가 말했습니다.

그런 다음 나와 그녀는 함께 복도로 걸어갔습니다. 그리고 그녀는 내가 운동장에서 무슨 일이 있었는지 그녀에게 말하게 했습니다.

그 후, 나는 루실에게 펜던트 목걸이와 스코티시 테리어가 그려진 스웨터를 돌려줘야 했습니다. 그리고 나는 그레이스에게 시리얼에서 나온 진짜 진품인 가짜 반지를 돌려줘야 했습니다.

그러고 나서 선생님은 쪽지를 하나 썼습니다. 그리고 그녀는 나에게 그것을 사무실로 가지고 가라고 말했습니다.

사무실은 학교의 대장이 사는 곳입니다. 그의 이름은 교장 선생님(Principal)입니다.

"네, 하지만 나는 오늘 저 아래층에 가고 싶지 않은 것 같아요." 내가 말했습니다. "그렇지 않으면 우리 엄마가 나에게 화를 낼 수도 있고요."

선생님은 그녀의 발을 툭툭 굴렀습니다. 그러고 나서 그녀는 내 손을 잡았습니다.

"어서 가자, 꼬마 아가씨. 쭉 걸어가렴." 그녀가 말했습니다.

그리고 그래서 그다음 나와 선생님은 사무실로 전진했습니다.

*전진하다*는 나를 너무 빠르게 끌어당겼다는 뜻으로 학교에서 쓰는 말입니다.

8장 나와 교장 선생님

학교 사무실은 무서운 곳입니다.

그곳에는 시끄럽게 울리는 전화기들이 있습니다. 그리고 타자를 치는 낯선 아주머니 한 명도요. 그리고 나쁜 아이들이 앉는 의자들도 한 줄로 놓여 있죠.

선생님은 나를 파란색 의자에 털썩 앉혔습니다.

"여기서 기다리렴." 그녀가 말했습니다.

"네, 내가 나쁜 아이는 아니지만요." 나는 나만 들을 수 있게 소곤거렸습니다.

그러고 나서 나는 내 스웨터를 머리에 뒤집어썼습니다. 그러면 아무도 나쁜 아이 의자에 앉아 있는 나를 보지 못할 테니까요.

그 후에, 나는 내 스웨터의 긴 소매를 통해서 살짝 훔쳐보았습니다. 그리고 나는 손 구멍을 통해 선생님을 보았습니다. 그녀는 교장실 문을 두드리고 있었습니다.

그런 다음 그녀는 그곳으로 들어갔

습니다. 그리고 내 심장은 엄청 쿵쾅거리는 느낌이었습니다. 왜냐하면 그녀가 나에 대해 이르고 있었기 때문이에요, 내 생각에 말이에요.

잠시 후, 그녀가 다시 나왔습니다.

교장 선생님이 그녀와 함께 나왔습니다.

교장 선생님은 고무공처럼 보이는 대머리입니다.

또한, 그의 손은 커다랗습니다. 그리고 무거운 신발을 신어요. 그리고 검은색으로 된 정장을 입습니다.

"잠깐 내 사무실에서 너를 볼 수 있을까, 주니 B.?" 그가 말했습니다.

그리고 그래서 그때 나는 그곳에 혼자 들어가야 했습니다. 그리고 나는 커다란 나무 의자에 앉았습니다. 그리고 교장 선생님은 내가 내 머리에서 스웨터를 벗도록 했습니다.

"그래서 이번엔 무슨 일이니?" 그가 말했습니다. "너는 왜 너희 선생님이 오늘 너를 여기로 데려왔다고 생각하니?"

"왜냐하면." 나는 아주 조용히 말했습니다.

"왜냐하면 왜?" 교장 선생님이 말했습니다.

"왜냐하면 그 그레이스가 바보 같은 입을 떠벌려서요." 내가 설명했습니다.

그러자 교장 선생님은 팔짱을 꼈습니다. 그리고 그는 나에게 처음부터 말해 보라고 했습니다.

그리고 그래서 나는 말했습니다. . . .

먼저, 나는 그에게 내가 할아버지 집에서 어떻게 하룻밤을 보냈는지 말했습니다.

"우리는 아침으로 맛있는 와플을 먹었어요." 내가 말했습니다. "그리고 나는 그중에 다섯 개를 먹었어요. 그런데 우리 할아버지는 내가 그것들을 모두 어디로 집어넣었는지 몰라요. 하지만 나는 그것들을 여기로 쏙 넣었거든요."

그러고 나서 나는 내 입을 벌려 교장 선생님에게 내 와플들이 어디로 갔는지 보여 주었습니다.

그 후에, 나는 그에게 밀러 할머니가 어떻게 병원에서 집으로 돌아왔는지 말했습니다. 그리고 할머니가 나에게 원숭이 남동생이 생겼다고 말한 것도요. 정말로 솔직하게 진짜로요.

"그리고 그래서 그다음에 나는 발표 시간에 아이들에게 말했어요." 내가 말했습니다. "그러자 쉬는 시간에 루실하고 그 그레이스가 나에게 예쁜 물건들을 많이 주기 시작했죠. 왜냐하면 그 애들은 원숭이 남동생을 처음으로 보는 사람이 되고 싶어 했거든요.

"하지만 저에게 안 좋은 일이 일어났어요." 내가 말했습니다. "왜냐하면 우리가 교실로 들어갔을 때, 선생님이 간식 쿠폰에 대해 알아챘거든요. 그리고 그러고 나서 그 바보 같은 그레이스가 자기 신발에 대해 바보 같은 입을 떠벌린 거죠. 그리고 그래서 내가 여기로 전진하게 됐어요. 그리고 나는 나쁜 아이 의자에 앉아야 했죠."

그러고 나서 나는 내 치마를 매만졌습니다. "끝이에요." 나는 친절하게 말했습니다.

교장 선생님은 고무공처럼 생긴 그의 머리를 문질렀습니다.

"주니 B., 아무래도 우리가 너희 할머니가 병원에서 집으로 돌아오셨던 시간에 대해 다시 이야기해야 할 것 같구나." 그가 말했습니다. "네 남동생이 원숭이라는 것에 대해 할머니가 뭐라고 하셨는지 *정확히* 기억할 수 있겠니?"

나는 나의 두 눈을 아주 꼭 감고 기억해 내려고 했습니다.

"네." 내가 말했습니다. "밀러 할머니는 그 애가 자신이 지금까지 본 것 중에 가장 귀여운 아기 원숭이라고 했어요."

그러자 교장 선생님은 자신의 두 눈을 감았습니다. "아아아." 그는 약간 조용하게 말했습니다. "이제 알겠구나."

그 후, 그는 살짝 미소 지었습니다. "있잖니, 주니 B., 너희 할머니께서 네 남동생을 아기 원숭이라고 말했을 때, 할머니는 그가 *진짜* 아기 원숭이라고 하신 게 아니야. 할머니는 그냥 아기가, 뭐랄까. . . 귀엽다고 하신 거야."

"나도 그 애가 귀여운 건 알아요." 내가 말했습니다. "그건 왜냐하면 모든 원숭이는 귀엽기 때문이에요. 나는 교장 선생님을 죽일 수도 있는 커다란 종류는 좋아하지 않지만요."

교장 선생님은 자신의 고개를 저었습니다. "아니야, 주니 B., 내 말은 그 뜻이 아니란다. 내 말은 네 남동생이 정말로 원숭이가 전혀 아니라는 거야. 그는 그냥 작은 남자 아기란다."

나는 얼굴을 찌푸렸습니다. "아니에요, 그 애는 작은 남자 아기가 *아니에요*." 나는 그에게 말했습니다. "그 애는 검고 풍성한 털에 기다란 손가락과 발가락을 가지고 있는 진짜, 살아 있는, 아기 원숭이라고요. 교장 선생님이 제 말을 못 믿겠으면 우리 밀러 할머니한테 물어봐도 돼요."

그리고 그래서 교장 선생님이 그때 무엇을 했는지 아세요? 바로 그건, 그가 할머니에게 전화했다는 거예요! 그는 밀러 할머니에게 곧바로 전화를 걸었어요!

그리고 그런 다음 그는 할머니와 이야기했습니다. 그리고 그러고 나서 나도 할머니와 이야기했습니다!

"저기요, 할머니!" 나는 엄청 소리치면서 말했습니다. "방금 여기에서 무슨 일이 있었는지 아세요? 교장 선생님이 내 남동생이 진짜, 살아 있는 원숭이가 아니라고 했어요. 원숭이가 맞는데 말이에요. 왜냐면 할머니가 나에게 그렇게 말했잖아요. 기억나죠? 할머니는 그 애가 원숭이라고 말했잖아요. 정말로 솔직하게 진짜로요."

그러자 밀러 할머니는 정말 미안하다고 말했습니다. 하지만 할머니는 남동생이 *진짜* 원숭이라는 뜻으로 말한 것이 아니었다고 했습니다. 할머니는 단지 그 애가 *귀엽다*는 의미로 말한 것이라고 했습니다.

바로 교장 선생님이 나에게 설명한 것처럼 말이에요.

그리고 그래서 그때 나는 마음속으로 아주 축 처지는 느낌이었습니다.

"네, 그럼 그 애의 검은 털은 다 어떻고요? 그리고 그 애의 기다란 손가락하고 발가락은요?" 내가 말했습니다. "그리고 동물 우리처럼 생긴 그 애의 침대는요? 그리고 그 애의 정글 친구들이 그려진 벽지는요?"

하지만 밀러 할머니는 계속해서 새로 태어난 내 남동생이 그냥 평범한 귀여운 아기라고 말했습니다. 그리고 그래서 결국 나는 할머니와 더 이상 이야기하고 싶지 않았습니다. 그리고 나는 전화를 끊었습니다.

그런 다음 나는 고개를 아주 푹 숙였습니다. 그리고 내 두 눈은 살짝 촉촉해졌습니다.

"에이 참." 나는 아주 조용히 말했습니다.

그 후, 교장 선생님은 나에게 휴지를 주었습니다. 그리고 그는 나에게 말했습니다. "유감이구나."

그런 다음 그는 내 손을 잡았습니다.

그리고 나와 교장 선생님은 9반으로 돌아갔습니다.

9장 돼지와 오리 같은 것

교장 선생님은 나와 함께 9반으로 들어갔습니다.

그러고 나서 그는 자신의 커다란 손으로 손뼉을 쳤습니다.

"여러분? 선생님을 봐 줄래요?" 그가 말했습니다. "선생님은 오늘 발표 시간에 있었던 일을 설명하려고 해요. 그건 주니 B. 존스와 주니 B.의 새로 태어난 남동생에 관한 이야기예요."

바로 그때 내가 싫어하는 짐 그 녀석이 그의 의자에서 벌떡 일어났습니다.

"그 애는 원숭이가 아니죠, 그렇죠?" 그는 아주 시끄럽게 소리 질렀습니다. "그럴 줄 알았어! 난 걔가 원숭이가 아닌 줄 알았다고!"

나는 그에게 커다랗게 주먹을 쥐어 보였습니다. "너 코에 이거 맞아 볼래,

이 멍청한 짐 녀석아?" 내가 소리 질렀습니다.

그러자 교장 선생님은 나를 향해 얼굴을 찌푸렸습니다. 그리고 그래서 나는 미소 지었습니다.

"나는 저 녀석이 싫어요." 나는 상냥하게 말했습니다.

그 후에, 교장 선생님은 크게 숨을 들이쉬었습니다.

"여러분, 주니 B.가 여러분에게 자신의 아기 남동생이 원숭이라고 말한 데는 그럴 만한 이유가 있어요." 그가 말했습니다.

"맞아! 그건 다 우리 밀러 할머니의 잘못이라고!" 내가 끼어들었습니다. "왜냐하면 할머니가 내 남동생이 *아기 원숭이*라고 말했기 때문이야. 그렇지만 할머니는 그 애가 *진짜* 아기 원숭이라는 뜻으로 말한 게 아니었어. 할머니는 그냥 걔가 귀엽다는 뜻이었대. 그런데 도대체 누가 그런 바보 같은 걸 알았겠어?"

교장 선생님은 또다시 나에게 얼굴을 찌푸렸습니다. 그러고 나서 그는 좀 더 이야기했습니다.

"있죠, 여러분." 그가 말했습니다. "가끔 어른들은 아이들에게 매우 헷갈릴 수 있는 말을 해요. 예를 들어 여러분이 내가 운 좋은 *오리(lucky duck)*에 대해 말하는 것을 들으면 어떨까요? 여러분은 내가 진짜 살아 있는 오리에 대해 말하고 있다고 생각할지도 몰라요. 하지만 운 좋은 *오리*는 그냥 운이 좋은 사람이라는 뜻이랍니다."

"맞아요." 선생님이 말했습니다. "그리고 우리가 누군가를 *일벌레(busy bee)*라고 부를 때, 우리는 그가 진짜 벌레라는 의미로 말하는 게 아니에요. 우리는 단지 그가 열심히 일하는 사람이라고 하는 거죠."

"저기요! 저 방금 하나 더 생각났어요!" 나는 매우 흥분해서 말했습니다. "멍청한 토끼(dumb bunny)도 마찬가지로, 진짜 살아 있는 토끼가 아니에요! 그건 그냥 평범한 아주 바보 같은 사람을 말하는 거예요!"

그러자 내 친구 루실이 손을 들었습니다.

"저도, 하나 알아요." 그녀가 말했습니다. "가끔 우리 할머니가 우리 아빠를 소파 위 감자(couch potato)라고 부르거든요. 하지만 아빠는 진짜 감자가 아니에요. 아빠는 그냥 게으른 사람이죠."

"맞아요, 그리고 저는 뚱뚱한 돼지가 아니에요." 나의 새 남자친구 리카도가 말했습니다. "하지만 우리 엄마는 내가 돼지처럼 먹는대요."

그 후에, 다른 많은 아이들 또한, 자기도 뚱뚱한 돼지처럼 먹는다고 말했습니다.

도널드(Donald)라는 남자아이만 자기가 말처럼 먹는다고 말했습니다.

그리고 울보 윌리엄은 새처럼 먹는다고 했습니다.

바로 그때 종이 울릴 시간이 되었습니다. 그리고 그래서 나와 교장 선생님은 서로에게 작별 인사를 했습니다. 그리고 나는 내 자리로 갔습니다.

그러고 나서 나는 루실에게 그녀의 빨간 의자를 돌려주었습니다. 그녀는 나에게 아주 친절했습니다.

"네 남동생이 진짜 원숭이가 아니어서 유감이야, 주니 B." 그녀가 말했습니다.

"고마워, 루실." 내가 말했습니다. "나도 마찬가지로, 너의 아빠가 진짜 감자가 아니어서 유감이야."

그런 후에, 우리가 집에 갈 때를 알리는 종이 울렸습니다. 그리고 그래서 나와 루실 그리고 그 그레이스는 손을 잡았습니다. 그리고 우리는 함께 밖으로 걸어갔습니다.

그런데 그때 아주 멋진 일이 일어났습니다!

그리고 그건 바로—내가 엄마 목소리를 들었다는 것입니다!

"주니 B.! 주니 B.! 이쪽이란다, 얘야. 아빠랑 엄마는 여기 있어!"

그러고 나서 나는 주차장을 보았습니다. 그리고 나는 엄마를 보았습니다! 그리고 그래서 나는 아주 잽싸게 엄마에게 뛰어갔습니다. 그리고 그런 다음 나와 엄마는 껴안고 또 껴안았습니다. 왜냐하면 나는 엄마를 하루 종일 보지 못했기 때문입니다!

그때 아빠가 차에서 내렸습니다. 그리고 그는 그의 품에 작은 노란색 담요를 안고 있었습니다. 그리고 그 안에 뭐가 있었는지 아세요?

그건 바로, 새로 태어난 나의 남동생이었어요!

그 애는 정말 작았습니다. 그리고 분홍색이었습니다. 하지만 그의 머리에는 검은 머리카락이 많았습니다.

나는 그것을 만졌습니다. 그것은 보송보송한 느낌이었습니다.

바로 그때 리카도가 지나갔습니다. 그리고 그는 나의 조그마한 남동생을 보았습니다.

"머리가 멋지다." 그가 말했습니다.

나는 환하게 미소 지었습니다. "맞아, 리카도." 내가 말했습니다. "그리고 또 그거 알아? 얘는 지독한 냄새도 나지 않아."

그런 다음 나는 차에 탔습니다. 그리고 나는 엄마에게 루실의 목걸이에 대해 말했습니다. 그리고 그녀는 나도, 목걸이를 하나 가질 수 있을 거라고 했습니다. 그러면 나는 그 안에 내 남동생의 조그마한 머리를 넣을 수 있습니다.

"네. 그리고 또 나는 분홍색 하이 톱 운동화도 갖고 싶어요, 부탁이에요." 나는 아주 공손하게 말했습니다.

"어쩌면." 엄마가 말했습니다.

"오 세상에!" 내가 말했습니다.

왜냐면 *어쩌면*은 안 된다는 뜻이 아니니까요! 그래서 그렇습니다!

그리고 그래서 그다음에 나는 담요를 들어 올렸습니다. 그리고 나는 한 번 더 나의 아기 남동생을 살짝 보았습니다.

"그래서 동생은 어떤 것 같니, 주니 B.?" 엄마가 말했습니다.

나는 정말 환하게 미소 지었습니다. "내 생각에 얘는 내가 지금까지 본 것 중에 가장 귀여운 아기 원숭이인 것 같아요." 내가 말했습니다.

그러자 엄마는 웃었습니다.

그리고 또, 나도 웃었습니다.

Chapter 1

1. C "Daddy and I have a surprise for you, Junie B.," said Mother. And so then I got very happy inside. Because maybe I didn't have to eat my stewie pewie tomatoes. And also sometimes a surprise means a present! And presents are my very favorite things in the whole world!

2. B Mother made me sit up. Then she and my daddy said some more stuff about a baby. "The baby will be yours, too, Junie B.," Daddy said. "Just think. You'll have your very own little brother or sister to play with. Won't that be fun?"

3. D Then Mother sat down next to me. "The surprise is that I'm going to have a baby, Junie B. In a few months you're going to have a little baby brother or sister. Do you get what I'm saying yet?" Just then I folded my arms and made a grumpy face. 'Cause all of a sudden I got it, that's why. "You didn't get me a darned thing, did you?" I said very growly.

4. A Daddy said that I owed her a 'pology. A 'pology is when I have to say the words I'm sorry. "Yes, but she owes me a 'pology, too," I said. "Because a baby isn't a very good surprise."

5. B Then Mother called me in there. And she said if the baby smells like a stink bomb, she will buy me my very own air freshener. And I can spray the can all by myself.

Chapter 2

1. A And guess what else is in the nursery? Wallpaper, that's what! The jungle kind. With pictures of elephants, and lions, and a big fat hippo-pot-of-something. And there's monkeys, too! Which are my most favorite jungle guys in the whole world!

2. C "This wallpaper looks very cute in here," I told them. "I would like some of it in my room, too, I think. Okay?" I said. "Can I? Can I?" "We'll see," said Daddy. We'll see is another word for no. "Yeah, only that's not fair," I said. "'Cause the baby gets all new junk and I have all old junk."

3. C "Of course I won't," I talked back. "Because it won't even let me hug you very good. And anyway, I don't even know its stupid dumb name." Then Mother sat down in the new rocking chair. And she tried to put me on her lap. Only I wouldn't fit. So she just holded my hand. "That's because Daddy and I haven't picked a name for the baby yet," she explained. "We want a name that's a little bit different. You know, something cute like Junie B. Jones. A name that people will remember."

4. D "Hey! I know one!" I said very excited. "It's the cafeteria lady at my school. And her name is Mrs. Gutzman!" Mother frowned a little bit. And so maybe she didn't hear me, I think. "MRS. GUTZMAN!" I hollered. "That's a cute name, don't you think? And I remembered it, too! Even after I only heard it one time, Mrs. Gutzman sticked right in my head!" Mother took a big breath. "Yes, honey. But I'm not sure that Mrs. Gutzman is a good name for a tiny baby."

5. B "I'm going to be the boss of this baby," I said to Tickle. " 'Cause I'm the biggest, that's why."

Chapter 3

1. D Yesterday a very wonderful thing happened! And it's called—I had pie for dinner! Just pie and that's all! That's because my mother went to the hospital to have the baby. And Daddy and Grandma Miller went with her. And so me and my grampa got to stay at his house. All by ourselves. And no one even babysitted us!

2. B After that, I opened up the 'frigerator. 'Cause I was hungry from playing, that's why. "HEY! GUESS WHAT? THERE'S A BIG FAT LEMON PIE IN HERE, FRANK!" I hollered. And so then Grampa Miller got down two plates. And then me and him ate the big fat lemon pie for our dinner!! Just pie and that's all!!

3. A Grampa looked all around the room. And also in the closet. "Nope. No hidey things in here," he said. After that he left on the hall light for me. So my

imagination wouldn't run wild. Except I still didn't sleep that good. 'Cause there was a drooly guy with claws under my bed, I think.

4. C And so this morning, my eyes felt very sagging. Only then I sniffed something that woke them right up. And its name was delicious waffles! Grampa Miller cooked them for me! And he let me pour on my own syrup. And he didn't yell whoa! whoa! whoa! After that, me and him played until it was time for kindergarten. Except before I left, the funnest thing of all happened! My grandma Miller came home!

5. A "You're just going to love him, Junie B.!" she said. "Your new brother is the cutest little monkey I've ever seen!" Then my eyes got very wide. "He is? Really?" I said.

Chapter 4

1. B "Grace is angry at you," said Lucille. "She said that she rode the bus today. And you weren't even there to save her a seat. And she had to sit next to an icky kid. Right, Grace?" Grace bobbed her head up and down.

2. D Then I tried to hold that Grace's hand. Only she quick pulled it away. "That's not very nice of you, Grace," I said. "And so guess what? Now I'm not going to tell you my special secret."

3. B After that, we had to sit down and do some work. It was called printing our numbers. Only I couldn't do mine that good. Because Lucille kept on talking to me, that's why. "Come on, Junie B.," she said in her whispering voice. "Tell me your special secret. I won't tell. I promise."

4. A I raised my hand way high in the air. "OOOOOH! OOOOOH!" I hollered real loud. "ME! ME! ME!" Mrs. shook her head at me. Because I'm not supposed to go oooooh, oooooh, me, me, me. She called on William. He is a cry-baby boy in my class. I can beat him up, I think. "William?" said Mrs. "Since you raised your hand so politely, you may go first."

5. A And so then William carried a paper bag to the front of the room. And he took out a jar of two dead crickets. Except for William didn't know they were

dead. He just thought they were sleeping.

Chapter 5

1. C "Guess what?" I said very excited. "Last night my mother had a baby! And it's the boy kind!" Mrs. clapped her hands. "Junie B. Jones has a new little brother, everyone!" she said. "Isn't that wonderful?" Then all of Room Nine clapped, too. "Yes, only you haven't even heard the bestest part yet!" I said very loud. "Because guess what else? He's a MONKEY! That's what else! My new brother is a real, alive, baby MONKEY!!!"

2. D "I SAID I'VE GOT A MONKEY BROTHER!" I shouted real louder. Then that mean Jim jumped right up from his desk. And he hollered, "Liar, liar, pants on fire!"

3. C Mrs. raised her eyebrows way high on her head. "Your grandmother told you that your brother is a monkey?" she asked me. "Yes!" I said. "She told me he has long fingers and toes. And lots of black fur all over himself!" After that, Mrs. kept on looking and looking at me. Then she said it was time for me to sit down.

4. A "'Cause guess what else? His wallpaper has pictures of his jungle friends on it. And his bed has bars on the sides. But I'm going to teach him not to bite or kill people."

5. B Then this boy named Ricardo—who has cute freckles on his face—said, "Monkeys are cool," to me.

Chapter 6

1. B "I don't want to play horses today," said Lucille. "I want to know some more about your monkey brother." "Me, too," said that Grace. Then Lucille pushed that Grace out of the way. And she whispered a secret in my ear. "If you let me be the first one to see him, I'll let you wear my new locket," she said.

2. C Except for just then I got a great idea! "Hey! Guess what, Grace?" I said very excited. "Since Lucille gave me something beautiful, now you can give me

something beautiful, too! And so that would be very fair of me, I think!"

3. A Then that Grace started smiling. And she took off her sparkly new ring. "Here!" she said. "I got it out of cereal this morning! See how shiny the stone is? That's because it's a real genuine fake plastic diamond."

4. D Then Lucille quick took off her red sweater with the Scottie dog on it. And she tied it around my waist. "Here!" she said. "Now I've given you two things! And so I'm still the winner." "Oh no you're not!" hollered that Grace. "Because I'm gonna give Junie B. my snack ticket for today. And so she can have my cookie and milk!"

5. B "Yes you do, Grace!" I said. "You do too have something else to give me! And their name is your new pink high tops!" That Grace stared at her feet. She looked very sad. "Yeah, only this is the first time I ever wore these," she said real quiet.

Chapter 7

1. D Before I sat down I looked at Lucille's red chair. Then I tapped on her. "I'm sorry, Lucille," I said. "But red is my favorite color. And so I would like that chair of yours, I think." Lucille looked very upset at me. "But red is my favorite color, too, Junie B." I patted her. "I know, Lucille," I said nicely. "But you still must give it to me. It's the rules."

2. A Just then, Mrs. Gutzman knocked on our door. And she came into the room with our milk and cookies. "HURRAY! HURRAY FOR MRS. GUTZMAN!" I shouted at her. "GUESS WHAT, MRS. GUTZMAN? I GET THREE SNACKS TODAY! SEE? I HAVE THREE SNACK TICKETS!"

3. C Mrs. raised her eyebrows. "Lucille? Did you give Junie B. your snack ticket today?" she asked. "Yes," said Lucille. "That's because she made me."

4. D Mrs. tapped her foot. "Please come get your snack ticket, Grace," she said. And so then that Grace walked to my table in just her socks. And Mrs. made squinty eyes at her feet. "Where are your shoes, Grace?" she asked.

5. B Then Mrs. wrote a note. And she said for me to take it to the office. The

office is where the boss of the school lives. His name is Principal.

Chapter 8

1. C The school office is a scary place. It has loud ringing phones. And a typing lady who is a stranger. And a row of chairs where bad kids sit.

2. B "So what's this all about?" he said. "Why do you think your teacher brought you down here today?" "Because," I said very quiet. "Because why?" said Principal. "Because that Grace shot off her big fat mouth," I explained. Then Principal folded his arms. And he said for me to start at the beginning. And so I did. . . .

3. B Then Principal closed his eyes. "Aaah," he said kind of quiet. "Now I get it." After that, he smiled a little bit. "You see, Junie B., when your grandmother called your brother a little monkey, she didn't mean he was a real little monkey. She just meant he was, well . . . cute."

4. A Principal shook his head. "No, Junie B., that's not what I mean. I mean your brother isn't really a monkey at all. He's just a little baby boy." I made a frowny face. "No, he is not a little baby boy," I told him. "He's a real, alive, baby monkey with black hairy fur and long fingers and toes. You can ask my grandma Miller if you don't believe me." And so guess what Principal did then? He called her, that's what! He called Grandma Miller right up on the phone!

5. D But Grandma Miller kept on saying that my new brother was just a regular cute baby. And so finally I didn't want to talk to her anymore. And I hanged up the phone. Then I bended my head way down. And my eyes got a little bit of wet in them. "Darn it," I said very quiet.

Chapter 9

1. B "You see, boys and girls," he said. "Sometimes adults say things that can be very confusing to children. Like what if you heard me talking about a lucky duck? You might think I was talking about a real live duck. But lucky duck just

means a lucky person."

2. D "Hey! I just thought of another one!" I said very excited. "A dumb bunny isn't a real alive bunny, either! It's just a plain old dumb guy!" Then my friend Lucille raised her hand. "I've got one, too," she said. "Sometimes my nanna calls my daddy a couch potato. Only he's not a real potato. He's just a lazy bum." "Yeah, and I'm not a big pig," said my new boyfriend Ricardo. "But my mom says I eat like one."

3. C Then I gave Lucille back her red chair. She was very nice to me. "I'm sorry that your brother isn't a real monkey, Junie B.," she said. "Thank you, Lucille," I said. "I'm sorry that your daddy isn't a real potato, too." After that, the bell rang for us to go home. And so me and Lucille and that Grace held hands. And we walked outside together.

4. A After that, the bell rang for us to go home. And so me and Lucille and that Grace held hands. And we walked outside together. Only then a very wonderful thing happened! And it's called—I heard my mother's voice! "JUNIE B.! JUNIE B.! OVER HERE, HONEY. DADDY AND I ARE OVER HERE!" Then I looked in the parking lot. And I saw her! And so I runned to her speedy quick. And then me and Mother hugged and hugged. Because I hadn't seen her for a very whole day! Then my daddy got out of the car. And he had a little yellow blanket in his arms. And guess what was in that thing? My new baby brother, that's what!

5. C "So what do you think of him, Junie B.?" said Mother. I smiled very big. "I think he's the cutest little monkey I ever saw," I said.

주니 B. 존스와 아기 원숭이 소동
(Junie B. Jones and a Little Monkey Business)

초판 발행 2021년 7월 1일

지은이 Barbara Park
기획 이수영
책임편집 박새미
편집 정소이 박새미
콘텐츠제작및감수 롱테일북스 편집부
저작권 김보경
마케팅 김보미 정경훈

펴낸이 이수영
펴낸곳 (주)롱테일북스
출판등록 제2015-000191호
주소 04043 서울특별시 마포구 양화로 12길 16-9(서교동) 북앤빌딩 3층
전자메일 helper@longtailbooks.co.kr
(학원·학교에서 본 도서를 교재로 사용하길 원하시는 경우 전자메일로 문의주시면
자세한 안내를 받으실 수 있습니다.)

ISBN 979-11-91343-09-0 14740

롱테일북스는 (주)북하우스 퍼블리셔스의 계열사입니다.